For Mom and Toekie

Andre van Heerden

An Educational Bridge for Leaders

60 brief passages on leadership through history

The Power of Integrity

ISBN: 978-0-473-17978-6

Published by The Power of Integrity Ltd.

PO Box 54 161, The Marina, Auckland, New Zealand 2144

www.powerofintegrity.com

Cover art: Detail from *Napoleon Bonaparte on the Bridge at Arcole* by Emile Jean Horace Vernet

CONTENTS

Introduction

Leaders and Misleaders – Finding a way beyond the worldwide crisis of leadership

Knowledge of human nature is the beginning and end of political education. Henry Adams

Why this book?

This book is not a leadership manual, but an effort to remedy the inadequacies of leadership manuals. Peter Drucker once referred to Xenophon's *The Education of Cyrus* as "Still the greatest book on leadership", and he made a very good point. Over many years, I have become convinced that a book like Orwell's *Homage to Catalonia*, on his experiences in the Spanish Civil War, or Simon Schama's *Citizens*, on the French Revolution, will teach you more about human nature and motivation, human perversity and potential, and therefore leadership, than any of the thousands of business leadership texts that flood our bookstores and libraries. That is why I believe that reading sixty short excerpts from history and classic literature will be of immense benefit to people who lead.

In a sense, this book is an attempt to put my money where my mouth is. After a decade of coaching leaders in business and government organisations along lines that clearly run against the grain of much that is being purveyed in the field of leadership development, I have found a chasm in the lives of most leaders I work with that I believe needs bridging. This chasm lies between them and the well-rounded education that alone will enable them to become effective leaders. This book does not pretend to be a multi-lane suspension bridge across to the Promised Land, a convenient, once and for all 'solution' to the 'problem' of their education, but merely a modest, even tenuous, rope-bridge that will help them get across the chasm to where the on-going educational development essential to effective leadership can be pursued.

The global crisis in leadership

If this claim for the book sounds arrogant, let me explain its origins in a little more depth. Apart from the many conferences and seminars where I have interacted with thousands of people in leadership positions, the corporate program I run has required me to form fairly intimate relationships with hundreds of others. I say intimate because processing 360-degree assessments and going one-on-one with participants to take them through what is often sensitive feedback, and then to work with them over the succeeding months in trying to address the issues that confront them, inevitably leads one to establish emotional bonds that transcend the normal working relationship, and often flower into genuine friendship. Then there are also the countless dinners and social functions where unguarded reflections, observations, and casual banter produce compelling indications of how people approach their role as leaders, and how they think about other people and leadership in general.

The overwhelming majority of these people have been emphatic in the view that there is a glaring lack of leadership in our society today – in their own organisations, in business generally, in government, the health sector, education, the professions, the police, and everywhere else you care to look. When I add this avalanche of opinion to the impressions drawn from my own personal experience as a teacher, a soldier, a policeman, an advertising copywriter in almost every business category you may care to list, a creative director, a marketing consultant, and a corporate mentor, I find that the same conclusion stands unchallenged in a rather bleak leaderless landscape.

The unimaginative and pusillanimous responses of world leaders to the current crises of war and the proliferation of armaments, globalisation, the economic disarray brought on by moral failure throughout the system, climate change, whichever side you may take in the debate, the future of fresh water supplies, social decay and cultural conflicts, and the persistent poverty that is inevitably attended by the exploitation of the more vulnerable people in our world, all tend to reinforce the conclusion: there is a very grave lack of leadership in our world today.

How can that be? There has never been as much dedicated literature on the subject; the management and leadership sections in bookstores are literally overflowing with volumes on how to mass produce leaders. A burgeoning multiplicity of university courses, corporate training workshops, and even school programs, all seek to either remedy or simply cash in on the very obvious deficiency. Moreover, in a perverse form of negative encouragement, political and business leaders provide an on-going sideshow that makes it clear to anyone who will take note, that there is an immense difference between promises and performance.

Yet, in the face of all these factors which are intended to cultivate a rich harvest of emergent leadership, we have instead only barren fields to contemplate. We have never been busier trying to produce leaders, yet we have never been so desperately short.

What has gone wrong?

In a nutshell, the basic error has been to believe that we can produce leaders simply by training people in the skills required, when, in fact, leadership can only be developed through genuine education. The radical distinction between training and education has been almost completely forgotten in the wake of scientific progress and modern technology, and their impact on culture generally, and school curricula and teaching methodology more specifically. In our schools and universities, what is now mostly skills-training with a vocational bias is blindly considered by the public at large to be an education.

Skills-training panders to our obsession with very superficial problem/solution thinking, and our not-to-be-denied passion for the quick-fix. It asks the question "What can you do?" and proceeds to provide skills targeted specifically to the narrow areas of need identified. Now let me emphasise that skills are obviously necessary and important to help leaders in their work, but they are insufficient to *create* leaders. I have worked with scores of people who have undergone all sorts of training in communication skills, strategy-development skills, conflict-resolution skills, negotiation skills and the like, who have been woefully inept when it came to leadership.

Moreover, looking at society as a whole, the rash of life-skills and people-skills programs on offer in all the nooks and crannies of the community has manifestly failed to prevent the slide into the social decay that afflicts all western nations today.

If leadership means inspiring, equipping, and enabling people to work enthusiastically together to achieve certain goals, then that demands qualities that can't be instilled in people through skills-training. Qualities such as vision, integrity, wisdom, creativity, compassion, and empathy, and a sincere desire to change something for the better, only grow out of a constructive and coherent, knowledge-based world-view, a robust strength of character, and a profound understanding of human nature. In other words, they are always and only the fruits of a sound and well-rounded education.

Ahhh...but what is a "well-rounded education"?

Let me stress that by education I don't simply mean what is supposed to happen at school, college, university, and in other formal programs.

Education, in essence, is a response to the question "What kind of person should you become?" Our word 'education' comes from the Latin 'educare' which means to draw out or lead from, suggesting the nurturing of personal potential to achieve the desired fruition. Education is about the whole person, about completeness and ultimate fulfilment; indeed, it is about the very integrity of the person. It involves his or her understanding and attitudes in relation to the whole of life, and it has to be a life-long process, nurtured in the initial stages by parents and teachers, but ultimately driven by individuals themselves.

The quality of an education is determined first by an adventurous and insatiable desire for knowledge, which parents and teachers are required to stimulate and cultivate, and thereafter, it is determined by the content of that knowledge. The content must cover the world and the place of people in it, providing insight into the part an individual might feel called to play. To be genuinely educational, content must provide knowledge and understanding of personal potential and human potential, personal goals and human achievements in arts and sciences, personal beliefs and human belief systems, personal political allegiances and human political alternatives, personal social arrangements and human social diversity, personal economic circumstances and human economic experiences, personal cultural commitments and the human cultural kaleidoscope. By definition, such content has to be drawn from the literature of past ages and civilisations as well as from contemporary texts.

Unfortunately, over several generations, content has been impoverished in our institutions of learning by three subversive factors: the ill-considered swing to skills-training and early specialisation, the misguided repudiation by the Enlightenment of the one thousand years of tradition, culture, and history that sprawls between antiquity and the Renaissance, and the contemporary obsession with 'relevance'.

Einstein worried about the pervasiveness of the first factor, declaring that "Perfection of means and confusion of ends seem to characterise our age." Education, as the ancients taught us, must lead us to three kinds of knowing: knowing that, knowing how, and knowing what. Contemporary training (it is simply wrong to call it education) is dedicated to the first two: knowing facts and knowing techniques; but it has nothing to offer when it comes to knowing what. What should I do? What should I think? What should I feel? What attitude should I take towards myself, and others, and to the world around me? To answer those questions requires me to have a proper understanding of myself and other people, and the world around me.

The second factor has led to the irony of huge gaps and costly prejudices in the minds of supposedly 'enlightened' people. Valuable texts from a massive expanse of the human story were ignored and forgotten, a totally misguided view of the history of Europe became entrenched, and a seriously flawed understanding of the history of science held sway for at least two centuries. How remarkable that some of the great modern philosophers handicapped themselves by never reading Aristotle, one of the towering geniuses of antiquity who was discredited in their minds merely on the grounds of his popularity in the Middle Ages. The effects of this Enlightenment obscurantism are still being felt today.

The third factor, 'relevance', locks people within the confines of their own little time and space, and denies them the obvious benefits of knowing about the vast epic of human history and endeavour, triumph and tragedy. It is a recipe for narrow-mindedness and a sure-fire prophylactic for wisdom. The very use of the word is a question-begging attempt to exclude certain content, deemed 'ideologically inappropriate', from the curriculum. How wrong-headed is that? The supposedly irrelevant meditations of Boethius on the consolation of philosophy helped preserve the ideals of the virtuous life and intellectual endeavour throughout the Dark Ages and beyond, for the benefit of all humanity. The supposedly irrelevant story of Cincinattus inspired Washington and his confidantes to reject the temptation of a Cromwellian military dictatorship or an American monarchy. The supposedly irrelevant classical studies of Greek and Roman antiquity helped Britain to administer an empire that spanned the world with a mere 1200 educated civil servants. The supposedly irrelevant study of Kant's Critique of Pure Reason inspired the young Einstein in his quest for a revolutionary explanation of the cosmos.

Nothing is more inimical to genuine education than 'relevance', ideologically defined.

The quality of our education depends also to a very large extent on how we use our leisure time. Leisure is a concept that has largely lost its meaning over the past century, as we have been sucked inexorably toward the whirlpool of total work, where people are regarded as functionaries rather than as persons. This is not the place to enter the controversial workplace issues of excessive workloads and the personal time-management conundrum, but the proper use of leisure time is fundamental to a genuine education, and therefore it is of major importance to all leadership development.

Significantly, the ancient Greek word for leisure gave us our word for school; it was meant as the time for personal development, mostly through the medium of good books and unpressured hours reflecting on them. When leisure becomes a stolen interlude of escapism in front of the television or on the Internet, or resorting to alcohol or drugs, or shallow and transient relationships that have little meaning beyond mere carnal release, then it ceases to be about personal development, and becomes a dehumanising contradiction. And while exercise and games, entertainment and hobbies, are all important elements of leisure, the reading of history and literature, of the type described by John Ruskin as "the books for all time" as opposed to "the books of the hour", remains the cornerstone of personal development.

What books will help provide a proper education?

The simple truth is that if we want to develop more leaders, we have to get back to a genuine education, the most important component of which is reading the right books. Now I am only too well-aware that for at least half a century, the question of what are the right books has sparked an often spiteful shouting match, and every attempt to draw up a canon of the great books has elicited shrill vituperation from ideologues. To unravel that post-modern Gordian Knot would take a book all of its own, but since I have been reckless enough to compile a book suggestive of a list of the right books to read, I am compelled to explain my position.

First of all, it so happens that I have very clear confirmation, based on personal experience, of the stories that inspire the thousands of different people, from a multiplicity of diverse cultures, that I have worked with ever since my early days as a history teacher. Secondly, there is now a deluge of empirical evidence that reveals the extent to which classic literature and history have enabled lower class people to enrich their lives spiritually, materially, socially, politically, and professionally, and copious quantities of research data that demonstrate, by way of a corollary, how in recent decades the lack of genuine education has locked people into impoverished lives with no hope of escape. Thirdly, there is equally imposing evidence of the part played by classic literature in producing the leaders who in the past two hundred years have helped oppressed peoples break the shackles of their servitude.

That said, in putting a book together to help bridge the gap between aspirant leaders and the educational enrichment they seek, I still had to address the question of the different worldviews that jostle against one another in our multicultural world.

If we are consistent with the understanding of education as the life-long process by which the intellectual and moral potential of a person is brought to fruition, then there are some definite guidelines against which all worldviews and all educational programs must be measured. They should come as no surprise to anyone, and indeed, I have found them embraced in all of the more than thirty different cultures of which I have had personal experience. So even though I know they are anathema to certain ideological standpoints, I declare them with complete confidence:

- A truly human worldview can only be built on a respect for the dignity of the individual human person. This is the basis of all the human rights we so casually take for granted in a world where most people are denied them. It is also the only meaningful foundation on which all human relationships can be built, in friendships, families, communities, workplaces and organizations, nations, and international affairs.

- A truly human worldview demands respect for the power of human reason, in spite of its patent limitedness and fallibility. We can only build a better world for all people through reasoned discourse on the things that separate us from others. Unless we acknowledge the purpose and benefit of this remarkable human attribute, common to all people, we are talking nonsense every time we open our mouths. It is interesting that those who tell you that there is no such thing as a common human rationality will use rationally-constructed, albeit specious, arguments to prove their point, in the firm conviction that all human beings should understand them.

- A truly human worldview must acknowledge that every human person is gifted with a unique potential, deserving of being nurtured and developed to lead it to fruition. This is the principle that under-girds the entire ethos of education, properly understood.

- A truly human worldview must affirm the personal freedom which is essential for self-fulfilment in each and every individual human being. However, freedom must be properly understood as "cosmic freedom", being free to choose those things we know to be good for ourselves, for other people, and for the world around us. Unfortunately, in modern western society, many people have come to believe instead in "chaotic freedom", that is, being free to choose to do what we like, perhaps, if need be, within the constraints of the law, even though history records countless examples of bad laws opposed by good people and good laws violated by bad people. "Cosmic freedom" says that we have a natural orientation towards choosing to do the right thing which just needs to be properly informed and developed. "Chaotic freedom" on the other hand says that human cooperation and community is only possible through external control. This philosophical argument has raged for 700 years, but the evidence of history strongly suggests that a truly human worldview would need to stand on "cosmic freedom".

- A truly human worldview must include an unshakeable commitment to an ethical and scientifically-informed stewardship of the environment. The world is the common home of all human beings and countless other species, and should be treated with respect and appreciation by all people.

It was in respect of the above ideals that I made the compilation of readings that follows. However, there were other considerations:

- I looked for brief passages, accessible to the general reader, which would enlighten, entertain, and inspire, and more importantly, whet the appetite for more, encouraging people to go to the books from which the excerpts were taken and paraphrased, and from there to many other great books that would further their education.

- The intention was to provide a broad sweep of the last 3000 years of history and culture.

- Obviously, texts about leaders or the qualities of leadership received precedence.

- Texts that demonstrated creative responses to seemingly intractable conundrums were especially favoured.

- I searched for texts that revealed the constancy of human nature and experience across all times and places.

- If the compilation is Eurocentric, it is because my own experience is centred on Western culture. Let me emphasise that the non-European texts included are not mere tokenism, but sincerely admired achievements that have influenced Western thought and inspired humanity at large.

- I make no apology for a bias toward texts that promote democracy, the rule of law, free enterprise, the traditional family, compassion and active support for the needy, and the brotherhood and sisterhood of humankind.

- Let me add a brief word on why I have chosen to paraphrase all the excerpts selected instead of using original passages or translations. In writing a book designed to encourage busy business people to buy and read the books of other people, I believed I was providing not just an educational service, but also a valuable marketing boost for many other authors and publishers. For that reason I did not anticipate any obstacles in getting approvals to use the chosen excerpts. I was wrong – the effort and frustration in trying to get just one approval convinced me that the task of acquiring sixty such certificates of permission would have taken many years, with no guarantee of success. In resorting to paraphrased excerpts, I am happy that for the purposes of this book, very little has been lost, and in some cases, easier accessibility for many readers may have been gained. I have given full credit to all the authors, and sincerely hope this book will encourage readers to go to the originals. If any paraphrase fails to do justice to the text from which it is taken, the sincerity of my regret can surely be gauged from the fact that I regard the authors concerned as essential beacons in any well-rounded education.

Without genuine, on-going education, we will never produce leaders, only misleaders. The alternative to using inspiration to get people to follow you is using force or lies, and of course, many so-called leaders throughout history have relied on force and lies to achieve their ends. It is interesting to note that the antonym of the word 'lead' is 'mislead', which means to deceive or to be untruthful. Dictators and tyrants, on the international stage, or in the boardroom, in the school, or in the home, are not leaders, but misleaders. They need force and lies to cover the dishonesty and perversity of their vision. Real leadership requires, above all else, personal integrity, which can only be built on education.

Does this mean that all properly educated people will automatically be effective leaders? Of course not. But only education provides the necessary foundations on which a person may choose to lead like they mean it, for the good of all, in pursuit of a better life for all. Wrong choices are common even among educated people, and the reality is that leadership failure is generally a failure of will rather than a failure of intellect. That is why the intrusion of ideology, or a nihilistic worldview, so often turns the prospective leader into a misleader. Genuine democracy demands of all citizens that they exercise qualities of leadership, in their homes and communities, in their workplaces, and in their free and conscientious participation in the political life of their nation.

This book can be read cover to cover, or by dipping in wherever, or by following a daily reading plan. There are sixty pieces drawn from classic literature and history, and also from contemporary authors, providing one reading a day for about two months. Everyone should be able to find the five minutes a day for the reading, but naturally, re-reading and reflection on the texts will pay additional dividends. Each piece is a door into another world, which you may wish to explore in the book from which it is taken, or in related books.

Appendix A at the back of the book has a useful reading list for further guidance. Appendix B has a list of some of the masterpieces of Western art from across the centuries, each recommended to be contemplated in stolen moments over a 24-hour period. Appendix C lists 30 pieces of music that will give you a better understanding of the importance of this achievement for all humanity. Appendix D recommends 25 movies and documentaries that will also help your on-going education.

After two months you will have poured into your mind a sprinkling of some of the finest literature and most influential history ever written. You will have negotiated the rope bridge across to a place where you should feel comfortably equipped to drive your further education all on your own.

Confucius considers the good, from
The Analects

The teachings of the Chinese philosopher, Confucius, have provided a guide for life to the Chinese people for 2500 years. What is more, people far beyond the borders of China have also found inspiration in the wisdom of this great sage, and he has exerted considerable influence in the western world. The on-going relevance of many of his teachings, coming to us today in a totally different time and place, is a salutary reminder of the fact that human nature has not changed with the passage of the millennia. The questions Confucius poses about the age-old philosophical puzzle of the One and the Many, about how we are meant to live in community with our fellow human beings, are crying out for answers today no less than they did in his own time. How should families, communities, and nations live together? How should those in authority conduct themselves? What sort of character should we seek for ourselves and others? Confucius wrote at a time of great social and political uncertainty, and ironically, he sought his answers from what he called "the ancients". We should take our cue from him, perhaps. The following paraphrase is taken from Book IV of the Analects.

The Master stated that it is the good that gives a community its beauty. If you are free to choose, but prefer not to live among good people, how could anyone consider you to have wisdom?

The Master pointed out that without goodness, no person can endure adversity for very long, and is unlikely to enjoy prosperity.

The good person feels at home with goodness, and pursues it knowing that it has practical benefits too.

The Master commented on the maxim: "Only a good person knows how to like people and how to dislike them." He said that even a person who only slightly yet sincerely seeks the good will dislike no one.

Everyone desires wealth and social status, but if they can only be had by violating one's principles, they should be spurned. Everyone hates poverty and nonentity, but if they can only be avoided by violating one's principles, they should be accepted. A virtuous person who rejects goodness doesn't deserve to be called a virtuous person because virtue and goodness are constant companions. Whether under pressure or duress, the virtuous person still holds fast to the good.

The Master noted that he had never seen anyone completely devoted to the good, nor anyone who really hated evil. A person sincerely committed to the good would never allow any other consideration to intrude. A person who really hated evil would be doing good so consistently that evil would never have a chance to seduce him. Has anyone ever managed to be completely good even for twenty-four hours? It seems highly unlikely. However, he had never seen anyone who gave up trying because he did not have the will to carry on; it might have happened sometime, but he had never witnessed it...

The Master stressed the point that a person who is convinced by the Way, but is embarrassed by the prospect of wearing humble clothing and eating plain food will not live up to its demands.

The Master explained that a virtuous person is not swayed by likes or dislikes in his approach to life; but always stands by whatever he identifies as the good…

The Master warned that people whose actions are governed by mere expediency will create on-going dissatisfaction all around them…

The Master maintained that the virtuous person is not opposed to holding public office, but does care about whether he has the necessary qualities for the position. He is not put out by a failure to get recognition simply because he is too focussed on doing the things that merit recognition.

The Master said that the Way has a single theme running all the way through it, and Master Tseng agreed. When the Master left the room, the disciples all asked what the Master had meant. Master Tseng told them that their Master's Way came down to two concepts: loyalty and consideration.

A look at *The Classical World* by Robin Lane Fox

Robin Lane Fox (1946 –) is a leading contemporary historian whose scholarly works have earned praise from both academic and popular quarters. He was educated at Oxford and now lectures at that pre-eminent institution of learning. Fox's impact on current historical studies has been substantial and it is to his credit that someone of his obvious erudition is still able to provide the general reading public with accessible and engaging books such as the one from which the excerpt below is reviewed. "The Classical World" is an absorbing read that can be enjoyed going from cover to cover, or simply by dipping in at random. Fox was an adviser to Oliver Stone for the film "Alexander". This report provides but a taste of his insightful appraisals and his scholarship.

Robin Lane Fox shows how it was to the great advantage of Sparta in the sixth century BC that the tyrannies in Greece were under strong pressure, due to the fact that the heirs of the first tyrants were even more tyrannical than their forbears, without providing any benefit to the people they ruled over. The coups that had brought the tyrants to power in many city states had been facilitated by conflicts among the nobility and the great social change that came with the introduction of the hoplites, heavily armed infantrymen drawn from the citizenry. Power-hungry individuals were able to take advantage of the temporary weakness of the noble families that resulted from these developments.

Once this military and social revolution became the accepted way of life, the nobles were able to work within it and form alliances to turn the tables on the autocratic rulers. Sparta proved to be a useful ally in ousting tyrants whose relevance had faded. But while there was a widespread belief that Sparta's socio-political arrangement was the best alternative to tyranny, there was little proper understanding of how Sparta was run. Nonetheless, aristocratic groups often conspired with Sparta to defeat tyranny, and Spartan influence spread throughout Greece.

The Greeks had come to equate tyranny with slavery, and hence to overthrow a tyrant was to win freedom from unconstrained despotism. Thus, in the polis or city state, it was not the slaves or repressed women who brought awareness of the ideal of freedom, but rather the personal experience of unjust tyranny on the part of the male citizens themselves.

Fox emphasises that political development in the polis had not been snuffed out altogether by tyranny. The roots of Greek democracy can indeed be traced all the way back to the aristocratic-tyrannical age of the sixth and seventh centuries BC. There were limits on the period of office in the case of magistrates, and officials were investigated at the end of their tenure. There were significant developments in legal procedure, and a public vote was used to elect officials, though it seems likely that this rudimentary ballot was controlled by the tyrants.

According to Fox, new political terms came into usage in the sixth century, as when citizens called for *autonomia* or self-government, which would allow them to run their own affairs. How far this socio-political freedom went was to be challenged, debated, and fought over for a long time. It seems the demand for

27

autonomia had grown out of awareness that, given the geography of Greece and its socio-political set-up, there were no external powers to repress it. Citizens of the polis went even further and demanded *isonomia*, translated as *legal equality*. Whether that meant equality before the law or equality in administration of the law is a moot point.

Fox relates how the tyranny of the Peisistratids in Athens, one of the few remaining, collapsed in 510 BC, prompting the search for new political guidelines. The contest between various aristocratic families went on for two years under what was left of the constitution of Solon, the great law-giver, and significantly, they agreed that henceforward it would be illegal to torture any citizen of Athens. The ideal of freedom was in the air.

In 508 BC, the Alcmeonids, a noble family that had led the way in expelling the tyrants, lost the supreme magistracy to a rival clan, and fearing political eclipse, came up with a novel expedient. When their rival assumed office, the leading member of the family, Cleisthenes, addressed the forum of all citizens, and proposed that a new constitution be established, investing sovereignty in the entire male citizen body. It was the moment of Athens' historic gift to posterity.

The 300 Spartans –from *The Histories* by Herodotus

The "Histories" of Herodotus, one of the earliest Greek historians, has proved a rich source of our understanding of the crucible of western civilisation for the last two and a half millennia. Though some scholars doubt the veracity of parts of this epic work, the broad sweep of his account of the struggle between the Greek city states and the Persian Empire has generally been accepted as a reliable historical account. His stirring narrative of the commitment and courage of the 300 Spartans under Leonidas in defending the pass at Thermopylae has inspired successive generations around the world. For several days, the Spartans and their allies from other city states embarrassed the much larger army of the Persian king, Xerxes, through their control of the pass. However, their fate was sealed when a traitor helped the Persians to outflank the Greek position. The following excerpt is a paraphrase from this classic story of leadership, both individual and cultural.

Xerxes waited for four days, fully expecting the Greeks to abandon their position and escape certain defeat, but on the fifth day they were still there, and their audacious defiance was taken as an insult by the Persian King. In a rage, he ordered his Medean troops to advance against the Greek positions, and to take prisoners so that they could be humiliated in his presence. The assault by the Medes was ferocious, but heavy casualties were inflicted on them by the Greeks as Xerxes' commanders kept sending more men in to replace the fallen. The battle raged throughout the day; when the badly mauled Medes were finally withdrawn, they were replaced by the King's Immortals, Xerxes' own elite Persian troops. The confidence of the invaders was renewed and Xerxes anticipated a quick and decisive end to the Greek resistance. However, the Immortals proved no more effective than the Medes in subduing the Greeks, and the pattern continued, with the outnumbered defenders of the pass actually having the advantage in the narrow battlefield because of their longer spears.

For the Spartans in particular this was a battle to relish; they were bred for warfare and up against them were largely inexperienced soldiers, more comfortable on parade than actually fighting. Their tactics completely outwitted their opponents, as when they suddenly turned and retired hastily to the rear as if they were beaten. The enemy charged after them exultantly, expecting to wipe them out, but just as the Persians thought victory was at hand, the Spartans would turn and launch another furious assault, inflicting further serious losses on Xerxes' army. Finally, the Persian commanders accepted the reality that their attempts to capture the pass were futile, and they reluctantly pulled their forces back from the battlefield.

Xerxes was at a loss as to how to overcome the tiny Greek army. Then, he was given an unexpected opportunity when Ephialtes, a man from Malis, hoping for a reward, revealed an isolated track over the hills which would allow the Persians to outflank the Greeks and surprise them at the pass. This traitor was responsible for the deaths of the courageous defenders of Thermopylae. The Persians made a forced march through the night along the deserted track that led through the mountains, and at first light they occupied the heights overlooking the 1000 Phocian soldiers who had been dispatched by Leonidas to guard that exposed flank.

An omen of the disaster that was to occur had already been given by the prophet Megistias. As a result, at a council of war many of the Greek commanders argued that withdrawal was the most sensible option. This caused a split in the Greek army which spelt its doom. Most of the Greek forces abandoned their positions at Thermopylae, and in the end Leonidas and the 300 Spartans were left to defend the gateway into Greece almost on their own.

Leonidas and his men knew that they faced certain death as the massive Persian army charged their position, and they decided to take the fight out into the open. In the days before the final assault, the Greeks had sought to control the narrow part of the pass, only advancing in brief surges to drive home any advantage they might have gained. Now they fought in the open. They took a fearful toll on the enemy, who were driven into battle by commanders wielding whips behind them, but eventually Leonidas fell, and that spelt the end of the Spartan resistance.

Their epitaph reads: *Go tell the Spartans, you who read. We took their orders, and here lie dead.*

A look at *History of the Peloponnesian War* by Thucydides

"The History of the Peloponnesian War" still stands after two and a half thousand years as one of the greatest works of history ever written. The author, Thucydides, fought in the long struggle between the Greek city states of Athens and Sparta, rising to the rank of general, and he has left us a remarkable example of a history written by someone who lived through the events described. In his own words, "My work is not a piece of writing designed to meet the tastes of an immediate public, but was done to last forever." Our understanding of ancient Greek civilisation would be impoverished without Thucydides' great masterpiece, which has generally been accepted throughout the ages as a reliably factual account of the conflict. The book is an entertaining and illuminating read for anyone interested in history, but more especially for leaders, in any field. In this paraphrase, he reproduces a famous speech by the great Athenian leader, Pericles.

We have a constitution which in no way tries to emulate the statutes of any other polis; we prefer to set the example rather than to follow others. The city state established by our constitution is a democracy, because it is set up for the benefit of all our citizens, rather than just a few. When it comes to settling private disagreements, there is full equality before the law for everyone; and we choose men for public office on their merits and according to their sound reputation in a particular area. A man's ability is what counts. Even if a man is poor, this does not disqualify him from serving the city, as long as he has the talent.

In public life we believe in personal freedom, and when trouble arises because of one individual's habits encroaching on others, as when our neighbour behaves selfishly in seeking his own pleasure, we don't react angrily or with those holier than thou attitudes that can cause so much friction. In our relationships we show mutual respect, and in public interactions we are discouraged from transgressions by a knowledge of the penalties they carry; we also have complete respect for people in authority and the laws, especially those that protect the person and his property. We are also mindful of those unwritten laws, the violation of which brings public disgrace.

What is more, we have all manner of recreation for the human spirit worn down by work, and we organise contests and celebrations throughout the year, and also provide attractive commodities imported from all over the world to afford more pleasure to people. We enjoy the goods of other countries as much as those we produce ourselves...

We admire beauty without extravagance, and we delight in intellectual pursuits without being soft. We regard wealth as a spur to greater achievement rather than as something for ostentatious display. Poverty is seen as nothing to be ashamed of, but we do think it a disgrace when a man does nothing to improve his position in life. All men are responsible for their own affairs as well as those of the polis, and while men make their livelihood in many different ways, they all understand the requirements of the polis. We are the only people who regard a man who refuses to participate in the affairs of the polis as worthless.

We exercise good judgment and accurate planning in our affairs because while others see discussion as an impediment to action, we believe that inaction or failure arises rather from the refusal to debate issues and policy. We differ from other peoples in knowing that we have to combine careful reasoning and decisive action to achieve our goals. In other states, courage arises from ignorance, and reasoned argument often causes them to hesitate. People who know through reasoned discussion what is harmful and what is beneficial, and who still stand firm in the face of danger, may be said to have the finest character.

When it comes to demonstrating good will, we are totally different to other peoples. We seek to gain friends not by accepting favours from them, but rather by performing acts of good will on their behalf. People who do good for others are much better placed to retain their good will as something of an obligation. On the other hand, if you are indebted to others, any favour you may provide will merely be regarded as the payment of what you owe them. We, of all people, show no hesitation in helping others, and give no thought to what we stand to gain, because we are confident in our generosity as free people.

Taken all together then, I can confidently say that our polis provides an education for the rest of Greece, and in my opinion, every one of our citizens, in every aspect of his life, can stand proud as lord and master of his own person...

Socrates discusses the good – from *Republic* by Plato

The English mathematician and philosopher, Alfred North Whitehead, once said that the whole European philosophical tradition consisted of a series of footnotes to Plato. Indeed, the influence of the Athenian philosopher on the development of western civilisation can hardly be exaggerated. Plato (427BC to 347BC) was born into an aristocratic family and was for a time a student of Socrates. In fact, Plato is one of the prime sources we have for our knowledge of his illustrious teacher who, unfortunately, never left any writings of his own to posterity. Plato's most famous work, "The Republic", like his other books, was constructed in the form of a dialogue, in which his leading character, Socrates, seeks to lead his students to understand ethical standards and the requirements for a stable and just society. The Socratic Dialogue remains as an indispensable tool for people sincerely seeking the truth in any matter – politicians take note! In this paraphrase, Socrates discusses with Adeimantus the need to have a clear understanding of what we mean by the term 'the Good'. Socrates is the first to speak.

"Now I am sure you have been told often enough that the idea of the good is the highest form of knowledge, and that all other things derive their value from this. You must certainly be aware that this is what I want to talk about, and you know that I consider our knowledge of it to be deficient. Moreover, such ignorance makes the rest of our knowledge, no matter how excellent, worthless to us. There's no point in owning something if you can't put it to any good use. Is there any possible value in possessing every other type of knowledge if you don't know what is good and what is not good?"

"Of course not."

"And surely you also know that the average person associates the good with pleasure, while more academic types consider knowledge to be the good."

"I suppose so."

"But these academics are unable to explain what they mean by knowledge, and are ultimately obliged to admit they mean knowledge of the good."

"Surely that is illogical."

"But they can't avoid it, because having criticised the rest of us for being ignorant of the good, they still go on and talk to us about it as if we did know. They glibly talk about 'knowledge of the good", taking it for granted that we know what they mean by the word "good"."

"Precisely."

"And as for those who equate the good with pleasure, they are also forced to admit their confusion, because there are pleasures that are known to be bad for us."

"That's right."

"And they find themselves saying that good and bad are one and the same."

"I guess so."

"So it's fair to say that the topic is fraught with difficulties."

"It certainly is."

"Yet is it not a fact that when it comes to justice or integrity, many people choose appearance over reality, whether it involves owner-ship, achievement, or reputation? But no one is content to possess something that merely appears to be good – in this case, we all seek reality and despise mere appearance."

"Absolutely."

"That means the good is the true goal of all our striving, and in our souls we are quite certain that such a thing actually exists, even though we find it hard to understand precisely what it is. And our lack of understanding impairs our true appreciation of the value of everything else. How on earth can we possibly trust leaders in our society if they are in the dark about this most crucial subject of all?

An excerpt from *The Education of Cyrus* by Xenophon

Xenophon (430 – 355BC) was an Athenian soldier of fortune and an author who had the distinction of being one of Socrates' students. His books on Socrates, together with the works of Plato, form the basis of our knowledge of the great philosopher. Xenophon's works are still widely read today. His "Anabasis" tells the story of the epic march of a group of Greek mercenaries across Asia Minor after an abortive attempt to help the Persian prince, Cyrus, overthrow King Artaxerxes. "The Education of Cyrus" is not about that hapless prince, but about the great Persian ruler of more than a century before. Cyrus the Great is remembered as one of the foremost models of the perfect ruler, and Peter Drucker referred to Xenophon's work as "still the best book on leadership". The essential lessons concerning human nature and motivation come to us still from every epoch in history

Thereafter Cyrus addressed other administrative concerns, and made several new appointments: tax collectors, financial controllers, infrastructure overseers, security officers, and stewards of the palace. He also created special positions for people to take charge of his horses and hounds, responsible for keeping the animals in excellent condition and ready for service at a moment's notice. However, in the case of the people he needed to help him in the administration and leadership of his expansive empire, he refused to entrust their personal development to other teachers, and took the task upon his own shoulders. He was deeply conscious of the fact that when it came to a time of war, he would have to appoint the leaders for the conflict from these specially groomed men. The officers for his cavalry and infantry would come from their ranks, and if he needed a general for an important mission, one of them would fill the post. Many of them would become satraps and governors of cities and countries, and also ambassadors, and he knew that diplomacy was the most effective way to achieve his goals without resorting to war.

He was prescient enough to know that matters would never go according to plan if his most important leaders were not of the finest quality. Success depended on them. This was why he took personal responsibility for their development, and he accepted that nothing should be required of them that he did not demand of himself. It is impossible to inspire others if one is not himself inspired to be the best he can be.

The more he thought about it, the more convinced he was of the need for leisure time if he was to meet the challenges facing him. Oversight of the revenues was vitally important, bearing in mind the enormous funds required to run such extensive territories, but Cyrus knew that preoccupation with the administration of different provinces and states would undermine his leadership of the empire as a whole. His reflections brought the old military organisation to mind, and he recalled how squads of ten men were led by a captain, how ten squads made up a company led by a company captain, how ten companies constituted a thousand, again with its own captain, and how ten thousands would also come together under a captain. In this way, a general could deploy hundreds of thousands of men by simply issuing orders to the captains of ten thousand, and no one would be without leadership close at hand.

Accordingly, Cyrus organised his finances and departments on this old military principle, and by communicating consistently with a handful of leaders he was able to influence the empire as a whole. Moreover, this ensured that he had more leisure time to devote to his own learning and development than a person in charge of a single household or the captain of a ship. Naturally, he taught his most senior officials in the bureaucracy to implement the same system in their spheres of influence.

The leisure achieved in this manner freed Cyrus to spend the time needed to develop the elite group of leaders to whom the future peace and prosperity of the empire would soon be entrusted. His first priority was to deal with the few misguided officials who became complacent and failed to turn up for their lessons. With the full knowledge of the king, one of Cyrus' companions would seize the offender's property, claiming it as his own. Then when the predictable complaint came in, Cyrus would make as if he had no time to deal with the issue. The offender was in this practical manner given a harsh lesson in the need for leaders to always have their priorities in order, and to make sure they met their responsibilities.

Alexander the Great, from Arrian's
History of Alexander

Arrian (c 95 – 180AD) was a Greek from Bithynia who became an officer in the Roman army. He is best remembered as the biographer of Alexander the Great (356 – 323BC) and his great work has come down to us almost in its entirety. Arrian remains our most valuable source of knowledge on the life and achievements of the remarkable Macedonian conqueror, and his book is still an exciting and informative read nearly two millennia later. In the two brief excerpts below, Alexander speaks about his achievements by way of a comparison with his father, King Philip of Macedon, and then Arrian gives his evaluation of this great military leader who has inspired millions across both the millennia and the continents. The fusion he set in motion between Hellenic civilisation and the oriental societies of Asia provided a major turning point in the history of the world.

"My father, Philip, left me nothing more than a few gold and silver cups and less than sixty talents in the treasury, and debts totalling around five hundred talents. I went ahead and borrowed another eight hundred and leading you all out from a land which failed to provide all you needed, I immediately took control of the Hellespont, even though the Persian navy commanded the sea lanes. After the victory of our cavalry against the satraps of

Darius, I annexed the whole of Ionia to your empire, as well as Aeolis, Phrygia, and Lydia. Miletus fell when I besieged it, and you reaped the benefit of all the other countries that willingly bowed to my authority. You enjoy all the riches of Egypt and Cyrene which I overcame without fighting at all, and you also have Syria, Palestine, Mesopotamia, Babylon, Bactria, and Susa, not to mention the wealth of the Lydians, the vast resources of Persia, the opulence of India, and the outer sea. You have become the satraps, generals, and tax collectors.

"Consider how little I have seen fit to retain in my personal possession other than the emblems of the emperor. I have taken nothing for myself. What treasures can you identify as belonging to me personally? Everything is held by you or kept in trust for you, because I see no advantage in holding on to these things for my own aggrandizement. I eat what you eat, and sleep in the same conditions; in fact, I don't think my food is as fancy as the cuisine some of you enjoy. And I remain vigilant so you can sleep peacefully." (Book VII.9)

Alexander died in the hundred and fourteenth Olympiad and the magistracy of Hegesias at Athens (323BC). Aristobulus tells us that he was thirty-two years and eight months old, and that his reign had been just twelve years and eight months.

He was an outstanding man in his looks and physique, in his enthusiasm for hardship, shrewd decision-making, courage, his love of virtue and danger, and in his piety. When it came to sensual gratification he showed admirable self-discipline, but as regards the delights of the mind, he was insatiable. He had the most amazing ability to choose the right course of action while it was still ambiguous, and was usually correct in making predictions from the information available. It was inspiring to see his skill in marshalling and equipping an army, in raising the morale of his men, giving them complete confidence, and sweeping aside their fears through his own bravery. In fact, once the most expedient course of action was clear, he showed unbridled audacity. If there was a chance of beating the enemy to the punch, he was always the man to take it, long before anyone else even had a notion of the possibilities.

He also distinguished himself as a man who stood by his treaties and undertakings, and one who could never be taken for a fool. When it came to money, he was extremely frugal in regard to his own satisfaction, but very generous in providing for the benefit of others.

If Alexander could be faulted for bad judgment due to pressure or emotion, or if he was seduced to accept barbarian practices that were excessive, I do not personally regard it as especially significant; we must just remember how young he was, his uninterrupted record of achievement, and the fact that it is men who seek favour rather than what is right, who are usually the associates of kings, and their influence can be evil.

But the sincere regret he showed for what he did wrong was exceptional among the kings of ancient times, and was typical of his virtuous character. (Book VII. 28-29)

Why democracies fail – from *Politics* by Aristotle

Aristotle (384BC – 322BC) studied for a number of years under Plato in the Academy, and many would argue he became a greater philosopher than his famous teacher. He was a Macedonian by birth, and later, for several years, taught the young prince who was to become Alexander the Great. Thereafter, he returned to Athens where he established his own school, the Lyceum, which attracted scholars from many parts of the civilised world. We are fortunate indeed that so many of Aristotle's works have survived, and his influence on Arab and Western philosophy has always been profound. He continues to be studied and referred to in schools of philosophy, government, business, and ethical studies even today, and reading any of his books is an enlightening exercise for anyone interested in humankind and how we ought to live our lives morally, socially, and politically. The paraphrased excerpt below shows how ancient many of our political issues are.

The most serious cause of revolution in democratic states is the unprincipled activities of popular politicians. Commonly they will make spurious legal claims on the property of the wealthy citizens, who naturally unite in opposition, because shared fear encourages even sworn enemies to close ranks. On other occasions these politicians instigate popular unrest, and examples of this type of activity are plentiful.

At Cos, the democratic institutions were overthrown when the wealthy citizens were pushed too far by mischievous popular politicians. At Rhodes, corrupt politicians tried to withhold money owed by the state to its naval commanders. The latter were incensed by being called before the courts again and again, and finally got together and brought down the democratic government. Similarly, the democracy at Heracles lasted only a short while after the colony was established because the high-handed measures taken by popular politicians forced the wealthy citizens to leave. These forceful men then put together an army and returned to put an end to the democratic regime. It was much the same in the dissolution of the democracy at Megara, where popular politicians banished wealthy citizens in order to seize their assets. This continued until those expelled became so numerous that it was easy for them to raise an army, defeat the popular army, and establish an oligarchy. It was no different at Cyme where the destruction of the democracy was caused by Thrasymachus.

By simply examining the evidence in these and other cases, it is clear that there is a pattern involved. Populist politicians seeking to get the mob on their side, engage in aggressive activities against the wealthy citizens, encouraging them to close ranks. The populists either make the wealthy divide their property as a means of financing public affairs, or they start making defamatory statements about the upper class to justify the confiscation of wealth.

In former times, a transition from democracy to tyranny occurred whenever a single person was both a popular politician and the military leader. In fact, of the early tyrants, most began their careers as popular politicians. This no longer happens for the simple reason that, whereas in earlier times the absence of eloquent speakers meant leaders were drawn from the army, today the spread of the skill of oratory enables men ignorant of military arts to rise to power with the support of the common people. Today's politicians are simply not equipped to lead military coups.

However, tyrannies were also more common in past ages because of the wide powers given to many public officials. For example, tyranny grew out of the office of the presidency at Miletus for the simple reason that too much power was vested in that position.

Of course, the fact that cities were so much smaller in earlier times is also a significant factor. While people were mostly dispersed across the rural areas, largely isolated and focused on their farms, ambitious men with military experience were tempted to pursue the option of tyranny. It was easy enough for them to win the support of the people, because the common folk generally hated the wealthy families. The revolt fomented by Peisistratus in Athens against the wealthy community on the plain is an example of this.

At Megara, when the herds of the wealthy were discovered grazing illegally on the land of others, Theagenes simply ordered his men to butcher them. In similar fashion, Dionysius won the support of the common people in the prelude to his seizure of power, by building a reputation as the accuser of Daphnaeus and the wealthy citizens.

Horatius – from *The Early History of Rome* by Livy

Livy (Titus Livius) was born in what is today northern Italy around 60BC. As a young man he moved to Rome, and there devoted his life to writing his monumental "History of Rome". His great work consisted of 142 books, and it is most unfortunate that 107 of the books have been lost except for fragments, extracts, and brief summaries. However, what we do have has still provided a rich source of knowledge and understanding of ancient Rome, and has been a major contribution to the culture of the western world. His account of the heroic actions of Horatius Cocles in thwarting the invading Etruscans has inspired people throughout western civilisation for two thousand years. Though some criticise Livy for moralising in his historical accounts of Rome, the 19th century English historian, Macaulay, believed that he showed how a great historian could actually reclaim material from the novelist.

As the Etruscan army advanced on Rome, people fled from their farms and took refuge in the city. The defending forces manned their posts, though the city walls in some areas were enough on their own, and of course, the River Tiber was also an obstacle for the enemy. The weakest point was the wooden bridge over the Tiber, and the Etruscans would have taken it, and the entire city, except for the courage of one man, Horatius Cocles, the remarkable warrior chosen by fortune to be Rome's shield on that fateful day.

Horatius happened to be on guard at the bridge when the Janiculum heights were overrun by the enemy. The Etruscans swarmed down from the crest, and the Roman defenders threw away their weapons and looked more like an ill-trained rabble than an army. Horatius took swift action, and tried to stop the rout by appealing forcefully to his terrified compatriots. He shouted warnings to them that there would be no hope if they did not stand and fight, pointing out that if the bridge was allowed to fall to the enemy, there would soon be more Etruscans on the Palatine and the Capitol than there had been on the western heights. Horatius urgently commanded them to quickly destroy the bridge by any means possible while he stalled the Etruscan surge on his own. With his sword and shield, he defiantly took up a position at the outer end of the bridge, with throngs of his panicked comrades still rushing past to escape the enemy. Standing ready for close combat, one man up against an army, he displayed an unwavering courage that forced the Etruscans to hesitate in amazement.

Two noblemen, Spurius Larcius and Titus Herminius, proud of their military reputations, rushed forward to support Horatius, and helped him weather the first wave of the Etruscan assault. But as the demolition teams had done their work quickly, and were calling the three to get back across to safety before it was too late, Horatius ordered his comrades to retire. Again he faced the best the Etruscans had to offer on his own, hurling defiant challenges at the frustrated ranks reluctant to exploit their full weight of numbers against the single defender on the narrow bridge. He taunted them for being slaves to the tyrant who was now trying to destroy the freedom of others.

After hanging back for a few minutes, each hoping that someone else would slay the Roman, their shame finally drove the Etruscan warriors to attack, and they launched their javelins at their quarry. But Horatius simply parried the spears away with his shield, and stood firm. Then as the attackers moved forward in unison, determined to crush the solitary figure barring their way, their charge was suddenly stopped by the thunderous collapse of the bridge into the Tiber and the loud cheering of the Romans on the other side.

The stunned Etruscans were further shaken as Horatius called on Father Tiber to protect him and his sword, and leapt fully armed into the torrent below. The missiles they hurled at him failed to find their mark, and Horatius swam strongly to the other bank of the river where his friends welcomed him exultantly. It was an amazing act of courage, perhaps legendary, but fixed in the memories of generations of Romans thereafter.

A statue of Horatius in the Comitium commemorates his brave deeds, and he was given as much land as he could encompass with a plough in a single day. In the hard economic trials that followed, many individual citizens paid personal tribute to the brave Horatius by foregoing their own comfort in order to support him and his family in their need.

The example of Cincinnatus, from Livy's *Early History of Rome*

Livy provides us with a remarkably vivid picture of early Rome, and leads us to a substantial appreciation of the culture that helped the city rise to the splendours of empire. The characters that crowd the pages of Livy's history are all object lessons on the demands, the duties, and the dynamics of leadership. For more than two thousand years of western civilisation, the story of Lucius Quinctius Cincinnatus was held aloft as an exceptional example of personal integrity as the essence of great leadership. The virtue of Cincinnatus inspired George Washington to resist the temptations of dictatorship and monarchy once the colonial armies had prevailed in the American Revolution. The crisis that brought Cincinnatus to power in Rome was the entrapment of a Roman army led by the consul, Minucius, by the Aequian army. An enemy victory would have opened the way for an attack on Rome itself, and the possible sack of the city. This paraphrased excerpt gives the gist of the story.

A fearful commotion gripped Rome, and the panic was as bad as if the city itself had been besieged by the enemy. The Senate sent for Nautius, but soon came to the conclusion that he would be unlikely to restore confidence. What was needed was one well-respected and forceful man to be appointed as dictator, and everyone was firmly in agreement when the name of Lucius Quinctius Cincinnatus was proposed.

At this stage I must address the commonly held view that money is everything in life, and that position and ability go hand in hand with wealth. Just consider the fact that Cincinnatus, the one man Rome was prepared to entrust with her survival, was at that very moment working a small three-acre farm west of the Tiber. The representatives of the city found him toiling in the fields, and after greeting him and offering a prayer for God's blessing on him and the republic, they requested that he put on his toga to hear what the Senate had to say. Taken aback, Cincinnatus asked if all was well with Rome, but he also told his wife, Racilia, to quickly bring his toga from their cottage. When she returned with the garment, he wiped the dirt and the sweat from his hands and face, and dressed himself. The representatives immediately saluted him as dictator and invited him to enter Rome in that capacity. They also told him of the fearful predicament that had befallen the army of Minucius...

Cincinnatus swiftly went to Rome and appeared before the people to make his decisions known. All the shops were closed and all private business was suspended from that moment on. All men of military age were ordered to report for duty before sunset in the Campus Martius fully-equipped. They were told to bring five days' ration of bread and twelve stakes. Everything was done as planned without delay...

The new Roman army's column of march was formed in such a way as to be ready for action instantly should the need arise. It left Rome with Cincinnatus at the head of the infantry and Tarquitius in command of the cavalry...The orders and encouragement flowed through the ranks of both divisions constantly, urging the soldiers to march with unrelenting vigour because there was no time to waste. It was imperative that they reached their objective that very night in order to relieve Minucius' army, which had already been under siege for three days.

It was midnight when Cincinnatus' army drew up close to the enemy lines at Algidus. The Dictator rode around the position in the dark to get as good an idea as he could of their dispositions...and he deployed his own men in such a way that the besieging Aequian army was caught between the Roman army they had entrapped and the one that had come to its relief...The fighting began in the dark of night...

Cincinnatus' soldiers heard the war-cry of their besieged comrades and knew that they too were required for action once more...Finding they were trapped between two fires, the Aequians quickly lost their nerve, and they pleaded with Cincinnatus and Minucius not to order a complete massacre, but simply to disarm them and allow them to retreat. Minucius left the decision to Cincinnatus, who accepted their surrender after imposing humiliating conditions...In Rome the Senate issued a decree inviting Cincinnatus to enter the city in triumph. The enemy commanders and the military standards paraded in front of his chariot, which was followed by the Roman army loaded with rich booty...

Cincinnatus resigned and went back to his farm after just fifteen days, though he had originally been appointed for six months.

The character of Hannibal – from Polybius' *Histories*

Polybius (c200 – 120BC) was a Greek historian sent to Rome as a hostage around 160BC. His assessment of the great Carthaginian general, Hannibal, is one of several sources that give us an insight into the mind of that famous conqueror. However, the estimate of Polybius deserves special consideration because of his reputation for objectivity, and because he was a personal friend of the grandson of the man who defeated Hannibal at Zama and effectively ended his career. He was with his friend when the latter presided over the final destruction of the city of Carthage around the middle of the 2nd century BC. Though he was a Greek, Polybius had a great admiration for Rome, and his assessment of the Roman constitution was a major contribution to political thought in the western world for the next two thousand years.

The problems relating to the invasion were discussed by Hannibal's council of war on numerous occasions. One of his friends, also Hannibal, but with the surname Monomachus (the Gladiator), suggested that there was only one way they would be able to get to Italy. When urged by Hannibal to explain, Monomachus bluntly stated that they would have to train the army to eat human flesh, and learn to do so themselves. Hannibal had no argument against the boldness or utilitarian nature of the proposal, but he refused to go along with the expedient, and his other friends supported him. It seems that the atrocities committed in Italy for which Hannibal was blamed were in reality the crimes of this other man, but one also has to take into account the force of circumstance in each case.

It does seem that Hannibal was rather too fond of money, as was his friend Mago, who was commander in Bruttium. My first intimation of this came from Hannibal's own people, and locals not only know which way the wind blows, as the proverb says, but also the characteristics of their countrymen. A much more in-depth assessment by Masinissa made clear that the love of money is widespread among the Carthaginians, and that Hannibal and his friend Mago were two of the worst culprits. Evidently the two of them had divided all manner of activities between them from the time they were boys. In Spain and Italy, each of them succeeded in taking control of many cities, sometimes by force and sometimes by deceit; yet not once did they participate in the same campaign. They were more careful in deployment relating to one another than they were in regard to the enemy, simply because of their greed. If one had been present when the other captured a city, there would have been an immediate conflict of interests, and any division of spoils between them was bound to be difficult because the two were of the same rank.

However, there were factors other than the influence of friends that adversely affected Hannibal's character. As my account will clearly demonstrate, force of circumstance was an even more corrosive element. When the Romans took control of the city of Capua, every other city, predictably, began to question their ties with Hannibal and the Carthaginians and to weigh up opportunities and justifications for renewing their allegiance to Rome. This crisis left Hannibal in a dangerous quandary. If he entrenched himself in any one region, he would make himself an easy target for different enemy forces bent on cutting off his movements. It would also be more difficult for him to maintain his control of the cities which were spread over such a vast theatre of operations.

Another option was to break up his army into smaller forces, but that would make each division more vulnerable, and he could only be personally in command in one place at a time. He found himself obliged to openly give up some of the cities and to pull his troops out of others because any insurrection would have cost him forces he could ill-afford to lose.

This led him to renege on some of the agreements he had entered into, sending the citizens away and taking their property as booty; this naturally incited widespread bitterness and led many people to label him as wicked and barbarous. Inevitably, these operations resulted in looting, murder, and excuses for violence on the part of both sides in the conflict because the remaining citizens were suspected of supporting the enemy.

For these reasons it is difficult to judge Hannibal's true character, but the Romans still remember him as a cruel man, and his own people as one who was too fond of money.

On good and evil – from *The Book of Wisdom* in the Bible

The Book of Wisdom was written by a Hellenized Jew living in the city of Alexandria in Egypt, probably in the first or second century BC. Tradition attributed the authorship to King Solomon, the son of King David, who ruled over the Jews when they constituted a wealthy and powerful state in the ancient world. Solomon, of course, was renowned for his wisdom, and would have been seen by the author as the perfect protagonist for the ideas presented in the book. The importance of the Jewish scriptures in the shaping of the western mind can hardly be exaggerated, and they are still a source of great wisdom and inspiration for people all over the world, regardless of religious beliefs. The Old Testament, quite apart from its massive spiritual significance for people of three of the world's great religions, contains a rich treasury of stories that continues to impact on art and literature everywhere. To ignore it is to jettison the very wisdom that is so badly needed in the world today.

Love uprightness you who are rulers on earth,
Be properly disposed before the Lord
And seek him in simplicity of heart;
For he will be found by those who do not put him to the test,
Revealing himself to those who do not mistrust him.
Perverse thoughts, however, separate people from God,

And power, when put to the test, confounds the stupid.
Wisdom will never enter the soul of a wrong-doer,
Nor dwell in a body enslaved to sin;
For the holy spirit of instruction flees deceitfulness,
Recoils from unintelligent thoughts,
Is thwarted by the onset of vice.
Wisdom is a spirit friendly to humanity,
Though she will not let a blasphemer's words go unpunished;
Since God observes the very soul
And accurately surveys the heart,
Listening to every word.
For the spirit of the Lord fills the world,
And that which holds everything together knows every word said.
No one who speaks what is wrong will go undetected,
Nor will avenging Justice pass by such a one.
For the schemes of the godless will be examined
And a report of his words will reach the Lord
To convict him of his crimes.
There is a jealous ear that overhears everything,
Not even a murmur of complaint escapes it.
So beware of uttering frivolous complaints,
Restrain your tongue from finding fault;
Even what is said in secret has repercussions,
And a lying mouth deals death to the soul.
Do not court death by the errors of your ways,
Nor invite destruction through the work of your hands.
For God did not make Death,
He takes no pleasure in destroying the living.
To exist – for this he created all things;
The creatures of the world have health in them,
In them is no fatal poison,
And Hades has no power over the world:
For uprightness is immortal.
But the godless call for Death with deed and word,
Counting him friend they wear themselves out for him;

With him they make a pact
Worthy as they are to belong to him.
And this is the false argument they use,
Our life is short and dreary,
There is no remedy when our end comes,
No one is known to have come back from Hades.
We came into being by chance
And afterwards shall be as though we had never been.
The breath in our nostrils is a puff of smoke,
Reason a spark from the beating of our hearts;
Extinguish this and the body turns to ashes,
And the spirit melts away like the yielding air.

Social decay - from *The Conspiracy of Catiline* by Sallust

Gaius Sallustius Crispus (86 – 35BC) was born in what is today San Vittorino, northeast of Rome. He entered upon a career in Roman politics and served both in the Senate and as a tribune. His political career was saved from charges of corruption by his friendship with Julius Caesar, who he served as an army officer in the Civil War. He was later appointed by Caesar as Governor of Numidia, but lost that position also on charges of corruption. Once again, his friendship with Caesar saved him, and he retired to his mansion in Rome to spend the rest of his days writing history. Only fragments remain of his major work on the history of Rome, but his accounts of the Jugurthine War and the Conspiracy of Catiline were greatly admired in the ancient world, and are generally accepted as valuable accounts of life in republican Rome.

Initially, it was ambition rather than greed that motivated men, and that flaw can easily be mistaken for a virtue. Recognition, official appointments, and authority are sought after by both good people and bad, except the former work with integrity, while the latter readily stoop to cunning and duplicity. Greed is another thing entirely – it comes down to a love of money, the mark of a fool. Greed poisons the mind of man, and can ruin him both physically and morally. Once set loose, greed can never be contained: the have-nots burn for what they are without and the wealthy always want more.

Following the military coup that saw Sulla become Dictator of Rome, that successful general proved to be a corrupt head of government, and there was a general upsurge in crime. Sulla's well-placed followers thought they could do as the pleased and take possession of whatever homes and estates caught their fancy, and this led to cruel mistreatment of citizens who had not supported the coup. Sulla exacerbated the problem by trying to buy the loyalty of the troops stationed in the Asian provinces. He relaxed the discipline Roman armies were famous for, and permitted high-living that would have scandalised his predecessors. This self-indulgence and decadence resulted in the loss of a true fighting spirit, and it was in Asia that the Roman fighting men first fell prey to the vices of sex and alcohol. They also developed a liking for works of art which they arrogantly seized from private homes and public buildings, looting temples and treating the subject cultures with contempt. These ill-disciplined soldiers would rape and pillage the enemy after every victory. It is a fact that even wise men are seduced by the fruits of success, so it is hardly surprising that these corrupted men acted as they did.

Once the Romans were persuaded that wealth was a sign of prestige and a short-cut to fame and high positions in government and the army, the old virtues ebbed away. People ridiculed poverty and honest living alike. Great wealth encouraged the younger people to waste their time and talents on luxury, corruption, and hubris. Grasping and prodigal, they showed no appreciation for what they had and no respect for the property of others. The traditional virtues of integrity and humility gave way to foolishness and excess.

It is an eye-opener to view their massive homes and compare the architecture with the temples constructed by our pious predecessors. In earlier times, reverence marked the homes of Romans.

In victory, they took away only the enemy's capacity for further conflict. Not so with later generations, who eagerly stole from subject peoples what earlier Romans had refused to take. They came to see oppression as the way to rule the empire.

There are some projects conducted by wealthy private citizens that have to be seen to be believed, such is the scale and extravagance of the excavation and construction. This was in my opinion a deplorable misuse of one's wealth. But every bit as disturbing was the wanton indulgence in promiscuity, drunkenness, and other temptations of the flesh. Men behaved like prostitutes, and women lost all respect for themselves and jumped into bed with anyone. They plundered land and sea to feed their gluttony, slept when they did not need to, and consumed for the sake of consuming. Prodigals who squandered their resources turned to crime, and their loss of character made self-control impossible. This led inexorably to the state of mind where they would do anything to keep getting and spending.

Advice for public officials from Cicero's *On Duties*

The Roman statesman and writer, Marcus Tullius Cicero (106 – 43BC), is remembered as the greatest of the Roman orators, and his surviving letters and works on ethics, politics, religion, and rhetoric, have exercised a profound influence on many of the greatest leaders in the history of the world. Cicero became a very successful lawyer, but his political career provided him with only sporadic achievements in an extremely turbulent period of Roman history. Nevertheless, his ambition and ability enabled him to achieve honours normally reserved for the sons of aristocratic Roman families, and he was elected Praetor in the year 66, and Consul three years later. But his enduring fame rests squarely on his astonishing abilities as a populariser of the great ideas of the ancient world, taking the treasures of Greek philosophy in particular, and rendering them accessible to a wider readership. He introduced many new words into Latin and hence was a significant influence on more modern European languages.

The most important thing in public office is to make sure that there is never even the slightest suspicion of corruption. In the words of Gaius Pontius, a Samnite: "If only I had been born at a time when the Romans started taking bribes, I could have brought the empire down."

He would have had to wait for several centuries because it is only in recent times that our national life has been afflicted by this disease. I suppose we can count our lucky stars that Pontius is not around today because from all accounts he was a formidable opponent. It has been little more than a century since Lucius Piso introduced legislation to penalise corrupt practices. There had been nothing like it before then, but in the years since, many similar laws have been introduced, each more severe than the previous one. Huge numbers of men have been tried and found guilty, and fear of the courts even provoked a very destructive war across Italy. Then the courts were suppressed and the rule of law along with them, and the subject peoples who support Rome had their lands and property laid waste and looted. The net result is that we can no longer trust in our strength, but have to rely on the weakness of others.

Scipio Africanus the Younger is justifiably lauded for his self-restraint in public life. However, he had many more impressive qualities than self-restraint, which after all belonged rather to the age in which he lived. For example, when Lucius Paullus took control of the vast riches of Macedonia, he filled the coffers of Rome to such an extent that the spoils of just one general allowed the government to abolish the property tax. At the same time, he kept for himself and his family nothing at all, other than eternal fame. Scipio the Younger was his son and followed the example set by his father when he destroyed Carthage once and for all. He took nothing for himself. His fellow magistrate, Lucius Mummius, likewise refused to make any personal profit from the conquest of the richest city in the world. His ambition was to decorate Italy and not his own home. Of course, this same virtue is precisely what did adorn his house in the most splendid way of all.

Let me repeat the message once more: greed is the worst of all the vices, and when it corrupts the most notable citizens and people chosen to head the government, it is particularly terrible. Men who take advantage of the affairs of state to feather their own nests are dangerously immoral, and their behaviour is sinful and criminal. Remember how Apollo made it known through the Pythian Oracle that there was only one thing that would destroy the might of Sparta, and that was greed. Every other nation that becomes wealthy and powerful should take heed of that warning. The right way for leaders to win the good will of their people is through demonstrating self-control and self-denial.

When politicians, are eager to present themselves as champions of the people, and propose measures to redistribute land, they mean to take the homes and property of other people. And it's the same when they call for the cancellation of debts. Men like that are eroding the very foundations on which our republic is built. Any politician who is prepared to act like that is attacking the very principle of justice. If formal property rights are allowed to be violated, the rule of law itself is swept aside. I will say it again: the essential function of any state or city is to always ensure that every citizen is protected in the free and uninterrupted enjoyment of his own property.

The Sermon on the Mount from the *Gospel of Matthew*

*The word "Gospel" derives from the Anglo-Saxon term "godspell" -
the good news of the redemption of humankind through the death and
Resurrection of Jesus Christ. The four Gospels are in agreement in all
essentials of the story, but the different social standpoints of the authors,
as well as the natural variety of human perspectives, explain some appar-
ent inconsistencies. Although Matthew wrote his work chiefly for Jewish
converts, his Gospel has always had a much broader appeal, and provides
detail in important areas that is not included in the other gospels. The
Sermon on the Mount is a call to all people to new life in Christ, and
remains a popular reflection even among non-Christians as a guide on
how to live one's life. Gandhi, for example, with his rich tradition in the
Hindu sacred writings, still considered the Sermon on the Mount as
something quite unique for the whole of humanity. This excerpt gives the
Beatitudes and then a portion of the rest of the sermon – reading the
whole thing in Matthew's Gospel will take you less than fifteen minutes,
and give you much to reflect on.*

1 Seeing the crowds, he went onto the mountain. And when he
was seated his disciples came to him. 2 Then he began to speak.
This is what he taught them: 3 'How blessed are the poor in spirit:
the kingdom of Heaven is theirs. 4 Blessed are the gentle: they

shall have the earth as inheritance. 5 Blessed are those who mourn: they shall be comforted. 6 Blessed are those who hunger and thirst for uprightness: they shall have their fill. 7 Blessed are the merciful: they shall have mercy shown them. 8 Blessed are the pure in heart: they shall see God. 9 Blessed are the peacemakers: they shall be recognised as children of God. 10 Blessed are those who are persecuted in the cause of uprightness: the kingdom of Heaven is theirs. 11 Blessed are you when people abuse you and persecute you and speak all kinds of calumny against you falsely on my account.

12 Rejoice and be glad, for your reward will be great in heaven; this is how they persecuted the prophets before you.

13 'You are salt for the earth. But if salt loses its taste, what can make it salty again? It is good for nothing, and can only be thrown out to be trampled under people's feet. 14 'You are light for the world. A city built on a hill-top cannot be hidden. 15 No one lights a lamp to put it under a tub; they put it on the lamp-stand where it shines for everyone in the house. 16 In the same way your light must shine in people's sight, so that, seeing your good works, they may give praise to your Father in heaven. 17 'Do not imagine that I have come to abolish the Law or the Prophets. I have come not to abolish but to complete them. 18 In truth I tell you, till heaven and earth disappear, not one dot, not one little stroke, is to disappear from the Law until all its purpose is achieved. 19 Therefore, anyone who infringes even one of the least of these commandments and teaches others to do the same will be considered the least in the kingdom of Heaven; but the person who keeps them and teaches them will be considered great in the kingdom of Heaven. 20 For I tell you, if your uprightness does not surpass that of the scribes and Pharisees, you will never get into the kingdom of Heaven.

21 'You have heard how it was said to our ancestors, You shall not kill; and if anyone does kill he must answer for it before the court. 22 But I say this to you, anyone who is angry with a brother will answer for it before the court; anyone who calls a brother

"Fool" will answer for it before the Sanhedrin; and anyone who calls him "Traitor" will answer for it in hell fire. 23 So then, if you are bringing your offering to the altar and there remember that your brother has something against you, 24 leave your offering there before the altar, go and be reconciled with your brother first, and then come back and present your offering. 25 Come to terms with your opponent in good time while you are still on the way to the court with him, or he may hand you over to the judge and the judge to the officer, and you will be thrown into prison. 26 In truth I tell you, you will not get out till you have paid the last penny.

27 'You have heard how it was said, You shall not commit adultery. 28 But I say this to you, if a man looks at a woman lustfully, he has already committed adultery with her in his heart. 29 If your right eye should be your downfall, tear it out and throw it away; for it will do you less harm to lose one part of yourself than to have your whole body thrown into hell. 30 And if your right hand should be your downfall, cut it off and throw it away; for it will do you less harm to lose one part of yourself than to have your whole body go to hell. 31 It has also been said, Anyone who divorces his wife must give her a writ of dismissal. 32 But I say this to you, everyone who divorces his wife, except for the case of an illicit marriage, makes her an adulteress; and anyone who marries a divorced woman commits adultery.'

On love, from the 1st letter of Paul to the Corinthians

St Paul (died circa 67AD) was the greatest of the early Christian missionaries responsible for the rapid dissemination of the Gospel through the Roman Empire. Born a Jew in the prosperous commercial centre of Tarsus in Asia Minor, he inherited Roman citizenship through his father, a fact that proved highly significant in his later life. He studied under the great rabbi, Gamaliel, and became a devout Pharisee, and actively participated in the persecution of Christians in Palestine. A decisive conversion experience on the road to Damascus led him to become a devoted follower of Christ, and the rest of his life was spent spreading the Gospel. His letters provide some of the most important theological texts of Christianity, and the excerpt below is probably the most famous description of love ever written.

If I speak in the tongues of men and of angels, but have not love, I am only a resounding gong or a clanging cymbal. If I have the gift of prophecy and can fathom all mysteries and all knowledge, and if I have a faith that can move mountains, but have not love, I am nothing. If I give all I possess to the poor and surrender my body to the flames, but have not love, I gain nothing.

Love is patient, love is kind. It does not envy, it does not boast, it is not proud. It is not rude, it is not self-seeking, it is not easily angered, it keeps no record of wrongs. Love does not delight in evil, but rejoices with the truth. It always protects, always trusts, always hopes, always perseveres.

Love never fails. But where there are prophecies, they will cease; where there are tongues, they will be stilled; where there is knowledge, it will pass away. For we know in part and we prophesy in part, but when perfection comes, the imperfect disappears. When I was a child, I talked like a child, I thought like a child, I reasoned like a child. When I became a man, I put childish ways behind me. Now we see but a poor reflection as in a mirror; then we shall see face to face. Now I know in part; then I shall know fully, even as I am fully known.

And now these three remain: faith, hope and love. But the greatest of these is love.

A look at *Medieval Essays* by Christopher Dawson

Christopher Dawson (1889 – 1970) was one of the foremost historians of the twentieth century, a man who helped pave the way to a vastly improved appreciation of the history and culture of Medieval Europe. He lectured at University College in Exeter, held a professorship at Harvard, and was twice invited to deliver the prestigious Gifford Lectures at the University of Edinburgh. In 1932 Dawson had the courage to denounce Nazi racism in a lecture in Rome attended by both Mussolini and Hermann Goring. He was a brilliant scholar and had the gift of conveying vast amounts of information and analysis in a fraction of the space required by his peers. This short paraphrase from one of his many wonderful books gives some indication of the penetrating insights of a great historian into the history of Rome.

Christopher Dawson explains how the cosmopolitan culture which spread across the entire Roman Empire had its roots in the genius of Greek civilisation. The example of the Greek city states had been taken up by different peoples throughout the Hellenic world, and in fact it had been part of the mission of Alexander the Great and his generals to impart the benefits of Greek culture to the conquered lands of Asia. New cities arose in Asia Minor, Syria, Palestine, Egypt, and right across the East as far as the Oxus and Indus rivers, in which political forms, architecture, and social and intellectual life reflected the Hellenic model. These new urban centres became in turn beacons radiating Greek culture across this vast swathe of Asia.

Naturally the life of the peasantry would have changed little apart from having to adapt to the demands of yet another conquering elite, but it was very different for the aristocratic and middle classes. Inexorably they were influenced and moulded by Hellenic culture to a greater or lesser extent, many becoming profoundly Greek in tastes and manners, others taking on at least the outward signs of the new culture. City life from India to the Adriatic became characteristically Hellenistic.

When Rome conquered the lands of the eastern Mediterranean she took up this Hellenistic cultural inheritance, but in her own pragmatic spirit. Initially, the Romans conquered purely to exploit, and commercial interests, financiers, slave-traders, and tax collectors swarmed into the conquered territories and took everything they could. It was typical of the Romans, from the high-born nobles engaged in commerce to the lowliest minions serving the large financial corporations, that they adopted this rapacious attitude. The final decades of the Roman Republic witnessed unrestrained exploitation across the Empire which impoverished the subject peoples and undermined the Roman state itself.

Dawson indicates that the crisis was resolved by the foundation of the Empire, with Caesar and Augustus crushing the corrupt oligarchy and self-seeking generals, and instituting the Greek model of enlightened monarchy. Prosperity returned to the widespread lands of the Empire, and the cosmopolitan urban culture described above gained new life over two hundred years of unbroken economic growth.

This lively socio-economic progress impacted subject peoples from Britain to Arabia, and Morocco to Armenia. New cities sprung up across the immense expanse of the Empire, and people increasingly took on the forms and manners of this refined culture.

North Africa in particular experienced a period of astonishing development, and the elegant ruins of this ancient civilisation still speak loudly of the glory that was Rome. Dawson refers to the example of Timgad in North Africa, a rather isolated and insignificant town, where there is evidence of public buildings and monuments that compare more than favourably with those of many modern cities, for all their wealth and technology. The people of Timgad enjoyed beautiful theatres and amphitheatres where free entertainment was provided, and stately porticoes and basilicas which facilitated both the business and the leisure lives of the citizens.

Dawson contends that this period of the early Empire has never been equalled for providing a civilised quality of life for so many people. He points out that the Hellenistic cities were built for the well-being of the citizens rather than being merely manufacturing or commercial centres, functional and no more. Rome itself provided the finest example of all, with the Greek democratic ideal of the right of citizens to be fed and entertained by the state taken to its logical extreme.

Even though Roman citizens had in the process lost the political rights enjoyed under the Republic, their rights to food and amusement continued to grow. The corn dole which had been restricted to around 200 000 citizens by Augustus, still required an enormous bureaucracy to administer it, and Egypt and Sicily, the main corn cultivation regions of the Empire, were required to service the needs of Rome exclusively. In time, other commodities were added to the dole, including wine, bacon, and oil; and cash payments, which had been resorted to even in Republican times, were extended by Augustus who made six payments to between 200 000 and 320 000 citizens.

Dawson also recounts the enormous commitment in time and money made by the state to keeping the people entertained, and most of the year was taken up by games and festivals.

On top of all this, the state committed massive sums of public money to public building projects, and while some were of real socio-economic value, like the aqueducts, others like the Colosseum speak of an extravagant pandering to the worst instincts of humankind. The ubiquitous public baths in particular grew in size and opulence right down to the fourth century AD, and Dawson points out that they became essentially "palaces for the people, of vast size, containing baths and gymnasia, lecture rooms and libraries, and adorned with the masterpieces of Greek and Hellenistic art."

Cities vied with one another for the honour of having the best public buildings, and wealthy citizens made huge contributions in this regard. What grew up was a culture that was materially rich but morally impoverished. The cult of success and self-gratification killed the old pagan religion, and while philosophy helped maintain a level of ethical standards among the elite, it could offer little to positively influence the lives of the great mass of society.

On self-control, from *On Anger* by Seneca

Lucius Annaeus Seneca (Seneca the Younger) (4 BC – 65AD) was born in Cordoba, Spain, and was brought up in the Roman Republican tradition. In Rome he became one of the greatest of the Latin Stoic philosophers, as well as a dramatist and also a political figure who was close to both the emperors, Claudius and Nero. He has sometimes been criticised for not living according to his own Stoic philosophy, and it is a fact that he was exiled on accusations of adultery with Claudius' niece. Nonetheless, his influence has endured throughout the ages and remains strong to this day. His writings remind us of the depth of understanding of human nature attained by the ancients, and even reading the plays he left us can be an illuminating cultural experience. Seneca was ultimately forced to commit suicide after he was arrested on suspicion of treason. The following paraphrased excerpt will be of interest to any contemporary student of human nature.

You only have to consider the consequences of anger and the terrible harm it does. No epidemic has been more costly for humankind. You see violence, the despicable venom of criminals, the tragic ruin of great cities and peoples, people of royal blood sold into slavery, homes burned to the ground, and wildfire that is not contained within the city limits, but spreads throughout the length and breadth of the land with scorching malevolence. Witness the vast lonely stretches of territory without a person to be seen, and remember that it was anger that denuded them.

Think of all the leaders recalled in the pages of history as victims of this pestilence. Anger slaughtered this one while he was asleep, took this one's life while he was enjoying a meal, mutilated this one in the senate house right in front of the a throng of witnesses, exposed this one to the barbarous violence of his own son, yet another being humiliated by a slave slitting his throat, and another being crucified.

And I have only focussed on the catastrophes suffered by individuals. Imagine if we ignored for a moment those who experienced the cruelty of anger as individuals, and contemplated instead the multitudes put to the sword, the ordinary innocents slaughtered by unleashed warriors, and the entire nations exposed to unrelenting savagery for refusing the protection of Rome or resisting our power…

The most practical remedy is to check anger at the very first spark, quelling the slightest hint of it, and being vigilant in keeping it in hand. Once it flares spontaneously, regaining control becomes increasingly difficult, and if we let anger out of the box and try to justify it, any rational explanation becomes futile. Once unleashed, anger has a life of its own that is completely unpredictable. This enemy of civil life has to be checked at the border, because once across, and let loose within the city limits, it will not observe the boundaries drawn by its prisoners.

The mind is not a separate entity that can consider the emotions in an objective way, keeping them contained within prescribed limits. Instead, it becomes transfigured itself into the emotion, and is soon incapable of restoring its own controlling function. Emotion and reason are never separate, independent realities, but are simply dispositions of the mind towards the good or the bad. This is why it is unlikely that reason will prevail once it has given in to anger. How will it transcend an unruly mix of all the worst emotions that have been given free rein?

Some people will object and point to those who are able to be in control even when they are angry. Are they saying these people never do what their anger tells them, or only do so sometimes? If the answer is never then it would seem that anger is not necessary in running our lives, even though the implication was that it is useful because it is stronger than reason. The point is crucial: is anger stronger or weaker than reason? If stronger, how could reason ever impose limits on it? Usually it is the weaker element that gives way. If, on the other hand, anger is weaker, then reason is competent to order our decisions and actions on its own, without the assistance of something which is inferior...

And as for the argument that anger is necessary in armed conflict, this is quite misguided, because a well-planned, controlled assault will always overcome a disorderly rabble. The barbarians are weakened by their anger in battle and lose their advantage of being physically stronger and hardier than we are.

On education, from *Institutes of Oratory* by Quintilian

Marcus Fabius Quintillianus (35 – 100AD) was a Roman rhetorician, lawyer, and writer, who served under many emperors in one of the most tumultuous periods of the Roman Empire. Born in Spain, he was later sent by his father to be educated in Rome. He did return to Spain for a time, but then settled down in Rome where he practiced law and served briefly as a consul. His only surviving work is the 12 volume "Institutes of Oratory", but there can be little doubt concerning the considerable influence he has exerted over the centuries. He helped shape the thinking of great men of letters like Augustine and Jerome, who in turn exerted a powerful influence throughout the Middle Ages and beyond. The Renaissance humanists made no secret of what they considered as the debt they owed Quintilian, and any theory of education today would be incomplete without reference to his ideas. The adherents of child-centred education trace their lineage back to him.

After twenty years dedicated to the teaching of young people, I was approached by friends who wanted me to write a discourse on the art of oratory. For some time I was reluctant because I was conscious of the fact that some of the leading Greek and Roman writers had already tackled the subject in well-known treatises prepared with meticulous care. Unfortunately, this perfectly reasonable pretext for refusing them only made them more determined. They argued that earlier writers on the topic had shown widely varying and even contradictory views, which served only to confuse people. That was why they felt it was up to me to either uncover the original ideas or at the least draw some definite conclusions on the variety of opinions. My decision to go along with them was based less on any confidence in my abilities than on the shame of refusing.

The subject was much bigger than I had thought, but as it happened I agreed to take on much more than the task as originally defined. I was committed to exceeding the expectations of my friends, but also determined to avoid covering the same ground as previous writers. Almost all the treatises written on the art of oratory were based on the assumption that the reader would be accomplished in every other area of education and needed only this crowning benefit. The authors either thought of the foundation subjects as insignificant, or dismissed them as someone else's responsibility, because in their minds, the professions are distinct from one another. But what is more likely is that they saw little reward accruing to them from covering subjects that might be necessary, but not prestigious, as for example in architecture, where the building rather than the foundations are admired.

For my part, the art of oratory demands everything that is necessary for the development of an orator, and will never be attained except by ensuring that the foundations are sound. Far from dismissing these preliminary stages which are essential for the more important things to follow, I intend to shape the studies of the orator from early childhood, just as if I were given responsibility for his entire education...

I aim at nothing less than the education of the perfect orator, who in the first instance must be a good man. Eloquence of the highest order is not enough; the quality of his character is even more important. We must reject the view that the principles of virtuous and noble conduct should be the exclusive province of the philosophers. The man who demonstrates the good character of a true citizen, who is well-qualified to manage the challenges of both public office and private business, and who can provide wise counsel for the nation, set it on a solid foundation through his statutes, and ensure justice through his judicial decisions, must certainly be the type of orator we are looking for.

That is why even though I acknowledge the need to draw on the well-established principles of philosophy, it seems obvious that they are closely related to the art of oratory, and need to be included in the book. It will be necessary to speak frequently of the virtues like courage, justice, self-control, and the rest, because they are relevant in every situation; and if they can only be profitably discussed through the use of intellect and articulate speech, is it not clear that wherever these qualities are in demand, our need for the perfect orator will be felt? Cicero demonstrates that these qualities are one in nature and practice, and are usually found in one and the same person.

On the mind, from *On the Trinity* by St. Augustine

Aurelius Augustinus Hipponensis (354 – 430AD) was one of the most influential philosophers of all time and his books are still avidly read and studied by millions all over the world today. Readers new to his books are generally pleasantly surprised by how accessible they are to the modern mind. Born and educated in what is today Algeria, Augustine for long time resisted his Catholic mother's pleas for him to become a Christian, and at one stage he even adopted the Manichean religion, which was heresy in the eyes of the Church. The gentle yet persistent influence of his mother, Monica, and later St Ambrose in Milan, led him finally to convert to Christianity, and he later became the Bishop of Hippo in Rome's North African province. The "Confessions" and "City of God" are two of the masterpieces among his many great books. This paraphrase is indicative of the power of his thinking.

Let's put aside for a moment everything else the mind knows about itself, and consider only memory, understanding, and will. It is in these three that we are able to see the abilities of the young: the more efficiently a boy remembers, and the more deeply he understands, and the more passionately he studies, the more we commend his ability.

However, when we assess a person's learning, we don't ask how efficiently he remembers, or how deeply he understands, but rather what the content of his memory and understanding is. And if the mind is to be commended when it is educated and good, then we must pay attention to not only what the person remembers or understands, but also what he wills. Note, it is not how passionately he wills, but first of all what it is that he wills, and only then how strongly he wills it. The mind that loves passionately only deserves praise when it loves those things that ought to be loved passionately.

If we reflect on these three things – ability, knowledge, and use – the first one must itself be considered in three ways: a person's ability in terms of memory, understanding, and will. The second one must be considered with regard to the contents of a person's memory and understanding as a result of the dedicated application of the will. However, the third one, use, lies entirely in the will, which manages the contents of memory and understanding, either directing them to further achievements or allowing them to lie fallow. To use something means to exert the power of the will over it; and to enjoy something means to use it with joy…

Memory, understanding, and will are not three separate entities with lives of their own; they constitute one life and one mind. Obviously, this also means that they constitute one being. Memory, for example, is referred to as life, and mind, and being, in respect to itself, but it is called memory in relation to other things. And this is also true of understanding and will, which have those names so that we can conceive them in relation to other things, yet in isolation each can be thought of as life, and mind, and being.

Therefore, we say that these three things are one – one life, one mind, one being. Whatever else they are individually called in respect to their own being can also be applied to them in their unity. But they are still three things that can be discussed in relation to one another. What is more, they are all equal, not merely each to each, but also each to all, because each mutually contains each other as well as all others. In other words, I remember that I have memory, and understanding, and will; I understand that I understand, and will, and remember; and I will that I will, and remember, and understand.

What is more, I remember as a whole my memory, my understanding, and my will. For any memory that I do not remember is not in my memory, and nothing is so completely in the memory as memory itself. What I remember is my whole memory. Likewise, I know that I understand whatever is understood by me, and I know that I will whatever is willed by me. And whatever I know, I remember. Therefore, I remember my entire understanding, and my entire will.

Moreover, I understand these three things as a whole. There is nothing intelligible that I do not understand, except those things that I do not know. And what I do not know, I can neither remember nor will. Therefore, it is logical that anything intelligible that I do not understand cannot be remembered or willed by me. Similarly, it follows that anything intelligible that I remember and will, I also understand.

A great emperor, from *The Life of Charlemagne* by Einhard

Einhard was born to parents from the lower ranks of nobility in what is today Germany, but what was in 770 part of the Kingdom of the Franks. He was educated at the monastery of Fulda and was later sent to the Palace School of the Frankish ruler, Charlemagne, with whom he became not just an adviser but also a close friend. Einhard was one of the many great scholars assembled by Charlemagne to promote learning and the arts throughout the Frankish Empire, and the cleric is rightly remembered as one of the architects of the impressive Carolingian Renaissance. Einhard's classic work on the life of Charlemagne offers a remarkable look at life in Europe when it was struggling to emerge from the nightmare of barbarism. The paraphrased excerpt below provides a compelling portrait of the great emperor, a man motivated by both his barbarian past and the Christian faith he had adopted.

Charlemagne was a strong man with a powerful physique, tall but not ungainly, as he was just seven times the length of his own feet. His head was round, and his striking eyes were surprisingly large. He had a long nose and a full head of white hair, and his countenance was bright and pleasant. Sitting or standing, he was an impressive, dignified figure. His short neck and slight paunch did not detract from this overall impression at all. He was strong on his feet and he moved with masculine grace. He spoke clearly but his voice lacked the depth for a man of his size.

The emperor enjoyed good health, though in his last few years he was afflicted by serious fever quite often, and he suffered lameness in one of his feet. However, none of that stopped him doing what he wanted, and he usually ignored his doctors. They really got on the wrong side of him when they told him that his favourite roast meat was bad for his health and that he should eat stew instead.

The Franks are among the greatest horsemen in the world, and Charlemagne spent a huge amount of time in the saddle, especially in the sport of hunting, for which he had a natural aptitude. Another favourite pastime was bathing in the thermal springs, and he took most of his exercise in this manner. He was such a powerful swimmer that few men could match him in a race. His love of swimming inspired him to build the great palace at Aachen where he stayed permanently in his final years until the day he died.

Charlemagne clothed himself in the traditional dress of the Franks. His undergarments were a linen shirt and linen pants, and over them he would wear long hose and a silk-trimmed tunic, shoes, and strips of cloth wrapped around his legs. In cold weather he covered his upper body with a close-fitting jacket made of otter pelts or ermine. He threw a blue cloak over his shoulders, and wore a sword at his side at all times, with the hilt and the belt made of either gold or silver. The only times he would carry an ornate, jewelled sword was on feast days or when meeting with foreign envoys. He had no liking for the fashions of other countries regardless of how attractive they might be, and he refused outright to even consider wearing them...Usually, his dress was much the same as that of the common people.

His eating and drinking habits provided a model of moderation, and in particular as regards the drinking. Charlemagne despised drunkenness and set strict standards for himself and his friends. Be that as it may, he struggled to go without food for any length of time, and when it came to fasting he claimed that it made him feel sick. He did not host great banquets often at all, usually reserving them for feast days; but on those occasions he would always invite a huge number of guests.

The main meal of the day was made up of four dishes over and above the roast meat that was his favourite food and which was brought in on spits by the hunters. Meals were generally accompanied by public readings or some other form of entertainment. Stories might be recited or the exploits of the ancients might be retold. Charlemagne derived a great deal of enjoyment from the books of St. Augustine and in particular those under the heading of *The City of God...*

He devoted himself to the promotion of the liberal arts in the Empire, and he showed sincere respect for prominent scholars and teachers. Many of these men were rewarded for their work with high positions in Charlemagne's administration.

The trials of kingship, from *The Life of King Alfred* by Asser

Asser was a monk and priest of St. David's in Wales in the turbulent ninth century. He was summoned to the royal court by Alfred, King of Wessex, in 885 and thereafter seems to have served as a close confidante of the king. Sometime after 892 he was made Bishop of Sherborne, and in 893 he wrote his "Life of King Alfred", which provides a remarkable contemporary source of information about the only English monarch to earn the cognomen "the Great". Alfred has inspired generations all over the world ever since his troubled but remarkably productive reign, and he remains a superb example of leadership for people in any field of endeavour. Always resolute and resourceful in the face of extreme adversity, he displayed his exceptional qualities as a soldier, scholar, administrator, and statesman throughout his long period as king. The excerpt paraphrased below gives a brief summary of some of the daunting challenges with which this wise and courageous leader had to contend.

King Alfred has steadfastly endured the suffering of many severe ordeals, notwithstanding the advantage of his royal prerogative. From the time he was just twenty until now, when he is at the age of forty-five, he has been constantly afflicted by a dreadful, unknown disease which gives him scarcely an hour's relief from either the pain or the fear of another attack.

Along with this malady, he has been troubled by wave after wave of attacks from foreign marauders, and he has had to defend the realm unceasingly from the beginning. Yet he has shouldered the burden magnificently, as can be seen from his many campaigns against the Vikings, and his dedication to the demands of government. Just consider the fact that he deals every day with many other nations spread out from Ireland to the Mediterranean lands – I have personally read letters to him from the Patriarch of Jerusalem.

And think of all the devastated towns that need to be restored, and new ones that need to be constructed. What about all the treasures beautifully fashioned in gold and silver at his command, and all the stone and wood buildings of the crown constructed on his instructions? Nor should we forget all the royal residences made of granite that have been relocated in more appropriate places under his orders. He has done all this while putting up with the disorder and apathy of his own people, who showed little inclination to contribute to the common good.

Once Alfred took the helm of the kingdom, with the help of God he single-handedly took great pains, like a superb pilot, to guide the potentially wealthy vessel to peaceful waters, despite the drained energies of his crew. He stayed resolutely on course, undaunted by the whirlpools swirling all around, and gently coaxed, drove, and directed his fractious subordinates to the desired destination. When his patience ran out, he did not hesitate to discipline people who disobeyed his orders. Treating popular folly and obstinacy with the contempt it deserved, he shrewdly motivated his bishops and earls and nobles, and the thanes he counted on so much, and also the reeves, in effect all those with positions of authority in the realm, to accept his will and work for the general well-being of Wessex.

Sadly, of course, there were occasions when all Alfred's forceful methods were thwarted by the laziness of certain people, or by the slowness of others to respond quickly in the crisis, and projects were not completed in time to serve their purpose. I refer here to

the fortified towns Alfred had wanted to be constructed throughout the country. When enemy raids suddenly flared up again,
there were many projects that had not even been started, and also
many more that were not yet finished. This meant that the ruth-
less marauders were presented with easy targets. It was then too
late for the victims to acknowledge their foolishness in failing to
follow the instructions of their king...

Alfred was extremely diligent in examining the details of all
judicial decisions made anywhere in the realm in his absence, to
ensure that justice had been done in every case. Whenever he
found a judgment to have been unfair or corrupt, he would re-
spectfully ask the official concerned, either in person or through
one of his trusted lieutenants, to give a full account of the court
proceedings. This exposed all the favouritism and bribery that
had been going on, and made judicial officers far more conscientious and just in the service they provided for the kingdom.

A look at the *Chronicle* of William of Malmesbury

William of Malmesbury (c1090 – 1143), born of a Norman father and an English mother, grew up to become a well-educated monk and a scholar and historian of major significance. His devotion to his studies and the writing of history, in which he was greatly influenced by the Venerable Bede, led him to pass by the opportunity to become Abbot of Malmesbury, and he remained there as the librarian and a scholar. In about 1140 he up-dated his two major works, "Gesta Regum" and "Gesta Pontificum", and began a new work "Historia novella", a sequel to the former, dealing with the period 1125-42, but this reads more like the first draft of a book rather than the final work. William's reliability as a historian is highly respected, and his reputation has continually reinforced the value he provides for the on-going contemporary studies of the people and times he wrote about.

This day in 1066 was calamitous for England because it replaced our rulers with foreign ones. The customs and manners of the Angles had prevailed in the country for centuries, evolving with the times. At first, the Angles were just barbarians in both appearance and conduct, savage and heathen. However, as they were slowly converted to Christianity, they turned away from their warlike ways and became very devout. Many spent their whole lives in service to the poor and in supporting the good work of the monasteries.

Unhappily, over time the devotion to education and religion waned and it was a very different society that faced the Norman invasion in 1066. An uneducated clergy found difficulty in articulating the words of the sacraments, and anyone who knew the basics of grammar was regarded with awe. The monks betrayed their vows in exchange for expensive clothing and fine foods, while the nobles, seduced by luxury and concupiscence, gave up going to church in the morning, preferring to simply call in a priest and go through the motions in their own homes.

Drunkenness at parties was commonplace, and often these debaucheries would go on for days. The dirty and rundown state of their homes was a telling comment on their decadence. By comparison, the Normans and the French lived in magnificent homes, exercising a thrifty and hard-working attitude. The vices that flow from debauchery obviously weaken the human intellect and will, and predictably, the Anglo-Saxons went into the conflict against William of Normandy with a hiss and a roar rather than any military acumen. That is why a single battle, won easily by the Normans, was enough to reduce them and their country to serfdom. Nothing is more ineffective than recklessness, because the initial fury quickly subsides when confronted by real strength of character and ability.

In those days, the English dressed in short tunics down to the knee, and they kept their hair short and their beards shaved. They enjoyed wearing an excess of gold bracelets on their arms, and they covered their bodies in tattoos. Gluttony was widespread, and the English often drank until they were sick. Of course, there were some who had not given in to these reprehensible practices – many clergy remained true to their vows and led a holy life, and many among the laity, from all levels of society, also tried to lead more productive lives.

On the other side, the Normans were in those days as they remain today, dressing with distinction, and discriminating in their eating habits, though not given to excess. They are a race bred for war; indeed they seem to live for battle. They display fearful aggression when they charge the enemy, but where raw power fails they are ready to use strategy or even bribes to get their way.

As I have said, they dwell in large castles with a degree of austerity. They are often guilty of envy in relation to their equals, and they generally strive to outdo their superiors. The defence they provide for their subjects is undermined by their propensity for robbing the unfortunate people as well. Though the Normans show great loyalty to their lords, the slightest insult can turn them into traitors. Paradoxically, they are generous to a fault, and they normally treat strangers with the greatest of respect. Intermarriage with their vassals is common in Norman society. The Norman Conquest revived religious observance throughout England; you now see churches in every village, and monasteries all over the country with an architecture that is clearly foreign.

On liberty, from *Policraticus* by John of Salisbury

John of Salisbury (c1115 – 1180) was a distinguished philosopher, historian, and churchman whose extensive writings provide a profound insight into the culture of medieval Europe. He was associated with many famous universities and schools, notably the great Cathedral school at Chartres. A close friend of St Thomas a Becket, he played a major role in trying to reconcile the Archbishop of Canterbury and Henry II, whose wrath he too had incurred, and John was a witness to the murder of Thomas in Canterbury Cathedral. John's great learning and energy enabled him to carry on a copious correspondence on literary, educational, and ecclesiastical topics with the leading scholars of the day. In this paraphrased excerpt, John demonstrates the depth of medieval thought on abstract subjects like freedom.

Liberty means being able to choose freely in all matters according to one's personal judgment, never hesitating to condemn what is immoral. Virtue is the only thing superior to liberty, that is, if the two can ever really be separated. In fact, sound thinking dictates that true liberty flows from virtue alone. This is why there is general agreement that the greatest of all goods is virtue, the only thing that can break the evil chains of slavery, and philosophers have held that we should be prepared to die for it because life would have no meaning without it.

However, complete virtue is impossible without liberty; virtue is impaired where there is no liberty. Therefore, a man's freedom can be measured by his virtues, and the extent of his freedom determines what he can achieve through his virtues. On the other hand, vices lead to slavery, driving a man to give in to people and things that are evil. And while being the slave of another person is deplorable, slavery to the vices is worse.

Is there anything more wonderful than liberty? Is there anything more attractive to a man who embraces virtue? Literature tells us that it has been the driving force of all good leaders, and that the only ones who ever suppressed liberty were the sworn enemies of virtue. Lawyers know that good laws are the ones promulgated to promote liberty among the people, and historians have a duty to keep alive the heroic actions taken in its defence. Liberty is a great gift, despised only by those who have the mindset of a slave.

Freely chosen actions and words avoid the opposing flaws of submissiveness and recklessness, and as long as they are virtuous they deserve to be commended. But using liberty as an excuse for rash and violent behaviour is obviously to be condemned; even though uneducated people might be taken in. Still, it is the duty of a wise man to place no undue restrictions on the liberty of others and even to be tolerant of the abuse of free speech. His guideline for action is when virtue is undermined.

Philosophers have described a tyrant as a person who oppresses the people through leadership based on force, and a prince as someone who rules according to the law. Law is a gift from God; the measure of fairness, a criterion of justice, a reflection of the divine will, the custodian of the common good, a bond of solidarity, a definition of obligations, both discouraging and destroying vice, and punishing violence and crime.

The law is attacked on all sides by either violence or dishonesty, and it might be said that it is mauled by the viciousness of the lion or deceived by the deceitfulness of the snake. In all the different ways this might happen, what is clear is that it is the grace of God which is being attacked, and that it is God himself who to all intents and purposes is defied.

The true prince champions the cause of the law and the liberty of the people; the tyrant on the other hand believes he has achieved nothing until he sweeps aside the laws and reduces the people to a state of servitude. The prince is a reflection of the goodness of divinity, and as such is to be loved and revered and greatly valued. The tyrant on the other hand is the reflection of evil and there is every justification to kill him. Tyranny springs from vice, and growing from a poisonous root it becomes a danger to everyone in society at large.

A saintly king, from Joinville's
The Life of St. Louis

Jean de Joinville (1224 – 1317) was born in Champagne, France, and succeeded to his father's title of Lord of Joinville while he was still just a child. He became a knight as the vassal of the Comte de Champagne and in 1248 joined the ultimately unsuccessful Seventh Crusade led by Louis IX of France against the Saracens. Joinville became a close companion of the king, who has been long remembered as one of the greatest of all the French monarchs, and in his old age the nobleman wrote his famous history of Louis' life. A shrewd and interested observer of human nature and culture, Joinville left posterity a book that remains valuable not purely as a historical source, but also as a vivid picture of life in the thirteenth century. This paraphrased excerpt reminds us of the perennial challenges faced by those who are given the reins of government.

In those days it was accepted practice for the position of Provost of Paris to be purchased by one of the wealthy freemen of the city, or anyone else who had enough money. Unhappily, it turned out that those who held the office, more often than not, simply overlooked crimes committed by their children or other family members, and the young miscreants soon took it for granted that they could get away with murder if they were related in any way to the provost. As a result, many injustices were brought to bear on the poorer people of Paris who found it impossible to obtain redress against the wealthy citizens, who were able to shower gifts and money on the provost.

During that period, when a person told the truth in court and, standing by his oath, refused to commit perjury in regard to the case in which he was called to provide testimony, the provost would quite likely castigate him and order him to pay a fine. As a direct consequence of the terrible injustices being done in Paris, many of the people from the lower classes preferred to leave this city situated in the king's personal domains and to go and live in places ruled by other feudal lords, where the provosts were not so corrupt. This led to the King's domains losing a large proportion of their population.

The net result of all this was that the criminal population in Paris and the adjoining territories became uncontrollably large. When Louis became king, he made it his first priority to learn the conditions under which the common people had to live, and whether their rights and interests were properly looked after. Once aware of the truth, he immediately prohibited the sale of the position of Provost of Paris, and made provision for a handsome salary to be paid to the person who undertook the responsibility of that important office.

Louis then went even further and revoked all the taxes and lev-ies that brought so much hardship to bear on the common people. He launched a campaign throughout his lands to identify honest and capable men who would restore the judicial integrity of the royal domains, ensuring both rich and poor were treated equally before the law.

One of the men who emerged from this quest was Etienne Boileau who became Provost of Paris. He performed his duties so honestly and thoroughly that most of the fraudsters, thieves, and murderers fled Paris, knowing that their kind was being hanged or imprisoned with alarming efficiency. Noble blood and bribes had lost their influence once and for all. The situation in the king's domains quickly recovered, and the population grew as people came to know that justice was being done for all. The economic consequences were significant and goods and property attracted better prices than ever before.

There was another decree issued by the king that went a long way towards improving affairs in the Kingdom of France, and which won the approval of many wise and respected people. The general thrust of it was as follows: *In all these concerns that we have enacted for the well-being of our people and our kingdom, we retain the right to clarify, amend, modify, or repeal in accordance with what we deem to be right.*

From the time he had been a boy, Louis had always shown compassion for the needy and the afflicted. He made it his established practice, wherever he might be, to invite a hundred and twenty poor people to his own home every day for a hearty meal. During Lent and Advent an even greater number of people were invited, and frequently the king himself served them the food.

An evaluation of Joan of Arc by Winston Churchill

Winston Spencer Churchill (1874 - 1965) was, with William Pitt the Elder, the greatest of Britain's war-time prime ministers, leading the country and the Empire through its darkest hour in confronting the Nazi Scourge. His leadership of the resistance to Hitler provided a model of resolute courage and resourcefulness in the face of seemingly insurmountable odds. Churchill was also a gifted writer and historian, and "A History of the English-Speaking Peoples", illuminating and entertaining on every page of four volumes, is already a classic text. His tribute to the inspirational Joan of Arc resounds with the awe her contemporaries must have felt in witnessing her remarkable, and well-documented, exploits. This paraphrased excerpt gives some indication of the extraordinary achievements of one of the most astonishing personalities to be found in the pages of history.

It was in this dangerous predicament that a liberating angel strode onto the stage, the most virtuous of all the defenders of France, her most celebrated hero, her most beloved saint, the greatest inspiration in her history, the peasant Maid of Orleans, the enigmatic Joan of Arc. She was a humble waitress in the tiny, isolated village of Domremy on the edge of the Vosges Forest, who began to have spiritual visions while tending the family sheep in the fields. Later in her trial by the English, she told how St. Michael had instructed her that God wanted her to lead the French armies in driving the English out. Naturally, Joan found this difficult to accept, but when the voices of the patron saints of the local parish, St. Margaret and St. Catherine, were added to that of St. Michael, she hesitated no longer.

At the tender age of seventeen, Joan travelled to the royal court at Chinon and was led into the great hall to meet the King who had been persuaded in his desperation to see her. To test her, the king mingled with the vast crowd of feudal lords and courtiers, but she singled him out without any hesitation, and this fed his vanity, because his claim to the crown had been contested on the grounds that he was a bastard.

As she conferred with the king, she revealed knowledge of confidential information that she could only have obtained from the French commanders or the saints whose authority she claimed to be acting under. She also requested to be given an ancient royal sword which she described down to the most minute detail, even though she could never have seen it before.

In 1429, the city of Orleans was hard-pressed by the besieging English, and Joan proclaimed that she was to lead an army to relieve the city. Dressed in ordinary armour she rode her horse at the head of the French force, and immediately renewed the confidence of the previously demoralised French soldiers, from the rank and file to the commanders.

On reaching Orleans, the Maid immediately ordered an assault on the besieging army, and personally led many of the attacks. There was a moment of panic in the French ranks when she was struck by an arrow, but when she pulled it out and resumed fighting, the French were inspired to redouble their efforts. Climbing one of the scaling ladders, she was thrown back into a trench, but even this failed to keep her from leading her men to victory. The

English strongholds wilted under the pressure and the siege was finally broken.

In 1430, the town of Compiegne rose in revolt when the French King ordered them to surrender to the English. Joan decided to try and save the townsfolk with a tiny force of six hundred men. Her courage and determination were not matched by some of the other French commanders in the fight, and they allowed her to be captured by the Burgundians who sold her to the English.

The records of her trial provide remarkable evidence for the truth about her career, and make it clear that the English were hell bent on executing her. She was burned at the stake in the marketplace of Rouen. An English soldier present expressed the fear that they had burned a saint; history proved him to be correct.

The story of Joan of Arc continues to fascinate and inspire people as a unique episode in history. The extant historical records mean that each generation can judge the Maid for itself, and the conclusions are not difficult to reach. She was the embodiment of the virtues that give humanity hope and strength: irrepressible fortitude, unbounded compassion, a resolute commitment to justice, and unshakeable faith. She willingly died to liberate the soil of her homeland.

Joan of Arc encourages people to reflect on the qualities of the true fighter, technically untrained, yet succeeding through sheer strength of character.

A look at *From Dawn to Decadence*
by Jacques Barzun

Jacques Barzun (1907 –2008) was one of the great teachers and cultural scholars of the past century, and a writer of rare genius. Born in France, Barzun was raised and educated in America. He received a PhD from Columbia University, and taught at that proud institution for many years. His last book, "From Dawn to Decadence", written when he was well into his nineties, deals with the past 500 years of western civilisation, from the Renaissance to our post-modern era. It has received widespread critical acclaim, and there is probably no better single volume history to provide one with a broad understanding of the world in which we live and the vast cultural heritage we often take for granted. The description below reveals some of the magisterial insights and illumination Barzun has given posterity.

Jacques Barzun explains how the Humanist generations of the Renaissance, committed to innovation, confident that they had stores of knowledge their forbears had lacked, and convinced that they were part of a new intellectual dawn, embarked on the re-education of the world aided by the printing press.

The printers produced a never-ending deluge of treatises on every art and science, from anatomy to arithmetic, from painting to metallurgy. Significantly, Latin was used less and less, because of the fact that printers were more at home with their native tongue, and clerics were no longer the only people who were able to read.

Barzun emphasises that this is not to deny the impressive intellectual achievements of the Middle Ages, but merely to show how diffusion of knowledge in Europe had formerly been restricted by socio-economic conditions. Guilds of artisans protected their intellectual property in the same way as corporations do today, and alchemists and astrologers also sought competitive advantage in strict confidentiality.

In the late 15th century, an emerging spirit of individualism and the waning of the guilds encouraged people to trust talent rather than secrecy to promote the value of their services, and the resulting cross-pollination led to an intellectual surge. Manuals publicised developments in technique in all areas of endeavour.

Barzun asserts that the flood of treatises provides a telling insight into the growth of a cultural movement. People are inclined to imagine such as being made up of a small group of geniuses supported by a throng of devotees, patrons, and assistants. However, the reality is that such a movement demands a great number of talented practitioners, the mass being a critical element in the surge of progress. And these practitioners have to be people of ability in their own right because even if they remain lesser lights or even unknown, they will contribute in significant ways to the overall intellectual development.

Important original ideas and pioneering efforts were often the work of people not fully appreciated by later generations. As integral and productive members of the general movement, people like this help maintain the spirit of innovation, and provide the ongoing stimulus for the geniuses among them.

Barzun notes that this understanding helps to explain the type of conditions that produce an exceptional era in the arts in an unexpected place at an unexpected time, and for a period all too brief. Contrary to popular wisdom, it is not economic growth, sagacious state subsidies, or even peace and stability – Barzun cites the example of Florence in its heyday being assailed from both within and without.

The main condition is the gathering of great minds in one place, through good fortune, rumours of exciting cultural developments, or some newly discovered technique. He then compares this cultural ferment with the spread of a spirit of revolution, with artistic rivalry and competition generating the wildfire of activity that results in exceptional achievements. Barzun argues that to produce a few geniuses requires hundreds of talented people. Cases of solitary genius are rare and such people are often scarred by their experience.

In eras of genius, the concrete comes before the abstract, works before ideas, but the theories that grow out of practice are still revealing in regard to artistic intention and the criteria by which they should be judged. Barzun stresses that these conventions stood for four centuries and should not be lightly swept aside by post-modern critics whose own purpose is to deny any purpose in art. The Renaissance treatises make it abundantly clear that in addition to his moral responsibility, the artist always had a clear aesthetic purpose, and that was to imitate nature.

Women rulers, in *Book of the Courtier* by Castiglione

Baldassare Castiglione (1478 – 1529) was born in Mantua to an Italian aristocratic family. He served as a diplomat in many of the courts of the Italian princes, but it was in Urbino that the conversations and background work were done for his classic book on courtly etiquette. "The Book of the Courtier" has left for posterity a remarkable first-hand commentary on Renaissance manners and society. This masterpiece has been translated into many languages and remains a valuable resource for students of the period to this day. It is a fascinating discourse that demonstrates the enduring truth that while manners and customs may change, human nature stays the same. The paraphrased excerpt below provides a sobering reminder for our chronologically snobbish age that enlightened attitudes were not invented yesterday.

The Magnifico said: "You can study any period in history to see the merits of women alongside those of men, and it will become clear to you that they have always been every bit as capable as men. Ignore for the moment the most ancient times and consider that when the Goths controlled Italy, one of their greatest rulers was a wise queen by the name of Amalasontha. The Lombards also had a remarkable queen in Theodolinda, and of course the Byzantine Empire had the formidable Theodora, the wife of the emperor Justinian. There have been many women rulers of enormous ability, for example the Countess Matilda, who we should ask Count Ludovico to tell us about. After all, she was a member of his family."

"I must decline the opportunity," the Count responded, "and leave you to do it. It is not right for a man to wax lyrical about his own family."

And so the Magnifico went on: "Think of all the outstanding women in history who came from this prestigious house of Montefeltro. And how many others came from the houses of Gonzaga, Este, and Pio? Even if you want to refer only to the current era, we will have no trouble in finding excellent examples, because they are all around us. But I am not going take advantage of the many able women present, because that might give someone the opportunity to claim you agree with me merely out of courtesy. Let's leave Italy for a moment, and acknowledge that our own era has witnessed the greatness of Queen Anne of France. Compare her in terms of justice, mercy, generosity, and virtue, with the kings, Charles and Louis, to both of whom she was married, and she is seen as their equal in every way. Think of Madonna Margarita, the daughter of the Holy Roman Emperor Maximilian, who has always displayed exemplary wisdom and justice in the government of her realm. Then, if we put to one side all the others, I ask you, Lord Gaspar, if you can name a single male ruler in this era or any other who might be favourably compared with Queen Isabella of Spain."

The Lord Gaspar confidently replied: "What about her husband, King Ferdinand?"

The Magnifico conceded: "It would be foolish to take issue with you on that suggestion – after all, the great queen did consider him as an eminently suitable consort, and obviously loved and honoured him in their marriage. Still, in my opinion the prestige he gained by marrying her was as valuable as the Kingdom of Castile itself."

The Lord Gaspar demurred: "On the contrary, Queen Isabella's fame rests in many ways on her husband's achievements."

But the Magnifico persisted: "The entire population of Spain – the nobility and the commoners, male and female, rich and poor – could hardly be mistaken in their appraisals all at the same time, and everyone agrees that there has simply never been a ruler of such integrity, wisdom, holiness, and generosity of spirit as Queen Isabella. Even though her fame across the whole of Europe is so exceptional as to be considered legendary, the fact is that the very people who lived with her and saw what she achieved for themselves, all insist that her reputation rested on her remarkable character and the things she did on her own account.

"One only has to review her achievements to be satisfied that this is true. For example, it is common knowledge that on her accession most of Castile was controlled by the great nobles, yet she quickly removed all their undue power from them, and was still able to command their on-going loyalty."

The Prince and honesty - from *The Prince* by Machiavelli

Niccolo Machiavelli (1469 – 1527) was an Italian diplomat and writer who produced a book on leadership that has provoked heated arguments from the time it was first published until the present day. Machiavelli's removal from office and brief imprisonment after the Medici overthrew the Florentine Republic no doubt coloured his thinking on statecraft, but the book itself reveals him as an advocate of all the evils that have afflicted politics and society throughout history. There is no doubt that "The Prince" gave encouragement to the absolute rulers of his own day as well as tyrants ever since, preparing the ground for Nietzsche's nihilism in the nineteenth century and the brutal totalitarianisms of the twentieth century. The paraphrased excerpt below highlights the essential challenge of leadership in all times and places, and the tempting choices that so easily result in a descent into misleadership.

All people acknowledge that honesty is commendable in a prince, conducting himself with integrity rather than deceit. However, experience shows that princes who have achieved great things have not usually put much stock in honesty. They have instead resorted to cunning and deceit in order to outwit others, and have got the better of those who stood on truth.

There are two ways to contend with others – by law or by force, the former being the way of man, and the latter the way of the animals. But as the law is often inadequate, the use of force becomes an option, and a prince must know how to play both the beast and the man. This lesson was given to princes in ancient times through stories of how Achilles was nurtured by the centaur Chiron, half beast and half man, and they could only conclude that it was necessary for them as rulers to be able to call up either nature as the need arose, since one on its own was not enough.

If a prince is thus required to behave like an animal at times, he must choose as his examples the fox and the lion. Lions are no good against traps, and foxes are defenceless against wolves, so a prince needs to be like a fox to spring the traps, and like a lion to intimidate the wolves.

It is simply judicious for a ruler to refuse to be bound by promises he has made when it is no longer to his advantage. If all men were absolutely good this advice would not stand, but since by nature men are bad and cannot be trusted to always act with integrity, it would be foolish for you to do so. You will find no end of plausible excuses for breaking your word. The records are full of examples of how treaties and agreements have been tossed aside by the dishonesty of princes, and the most successful have generally been those who knew how to play the fox.

Of course, you must be an expert at disguising this side of your character, being at all times capable of convincing others that you are clearly in the right, whatever the issue may be. This is not difficult, because men are mostly stupid and so enslaved by their current needs and desires, that the fox will always be able to manipulate them by means of deceit.

Accordingly, while there is no real need for a prince to have all the virtues I have spoken about, it is essential that he appears to possess them all. It would be foolish for a prince, and especially a new one, to conduct himself always with the virtues for which men are praised. There will be times when, in order to preserve the state, he will be forced to take action that violates honesty, friendship, compassion, and religious belief. His mind should be ready at all times to change with shifting circumstances and clear necessity; if he can do good without disadvantage, fine, but when forced to do bad, he must never shrink from the task.

This is why every word a prince utters should suggest that he is a paragon of the five virtues mentioned earlier: mercy, honesty, compassion, integrity, and religious commitment. People must believe that he is virtuous, even though he is not.

The last quality mentioned, in particular, is essential for a prince to appear to possess, bearing in mind that perception is more powerful than reality. Everybody sees you, but very few actually come into direct contact. All the people can form an opinion on what they see, but very few can really know what kind of person you are at heart. And those few people who know the truth are unlikely to contradict the opinion of the majority, backed as it is by the power of the government.

When it is injudicious to challenge a man's actions, especially those of a prince, people will tend to make up their minds according to the results that flow from those actions.

On conscience – Thomas More in the Tower of London

Sir Thomas More (1478–1535) is remembered today as the hero of Robert Bolt's superb drama, "A Man for All Seasons", and is justifiably admired by people from all sides of the political spectrum. The stand he took against the tyranny of Henry VIII as a matter of personal conscience has challenged every generation since then, and remains as a testimony against arbitrary government. More was also the author of "Utopia", the famous book on the establishment of the perfect state, which he wisely called "Nowhere". His views were so inimical to unjust government that the book was only published some years after his death. Lawyer and judge, diplomat and politician, man of wealth and man of faith, More was greatly admired by many of the leading intellectuals of the Renaissance in Europe. However, his lasting fame rests on the unwavering determination he showed in staying true to his conscience. The paraphrased excerpt below is from a letter written by More to his daughter Meg shortly before his execution.

Since it is likely, my dear daughter, that you have heard, or will do so soon, that the Council was here today to speak with me again, I thought I had better let you know how matters stand. In short, things stand much as they did before, and as far as I can see, it is their express intention to force me to state explicitly whether I accept the statute as lawful or not.

Present were my Lord of Canterbury, my Lord Chancellor, my Lord of Suffolk, my Lord of Wiltshire, and Master Secretary. As soon as I was brought before them, Master Secretary ran through what had been reported to His Royal Highness about what the Council had said to me and what answers I had given at the last meeting. I believe his account was a fair representation, and I thanked him most cordially for his efforts.

He then added that the King was far from satisfied with my response, and felt that by my stance I was being a negative and harmful influence throughout the country. He said that the King accused me of being obstinate and malevolent towards him when it was my duty to simply be his loyal subject.

Accordingly, the King had sent the Council in his name to test my allegiance and to command me to give a clear and definitive answer as to whether I thought the statute was lawful or not. I was told to either acknowledge that it was lawful for the King to be Supreme Head of the Church of England, or to express my evil intentions openly.

My reply was that I had no evil intentions, and therefore had none I could express. As to the question itself, I said I could give no other answer than that I had already given, which Master Secretary had been over in his report. I made known the deep sadness I felt hearing that the King had such a negative opinion of me...However, I thanked God that through the clearness of my own conscience, though I might be subjected to pain, still no harm would befall me, since in such a case a man might lose his head without coming to harm.

I was firm in my belief that I am guilty of no evil intent, and have from the beginning always put God first and then the King, according to the lesson taught to me by the King himself when I first entered his service...

111

Both the Lord Chancellor and Master Secretary then said that the King could force me, according to the law, to give a clear statement one way or the other. I answered that while I could not dispute the King's authority and what he might do, it seemed to me (though I was open to correction) that such compulsion would be difficult. If my conscience were opposed to the statute (and I was speaking only hypothetically), but I chose to neither do nor say anything against it, there would be great difficulty in forcing me to openly support it against my conscience to the loss of my soul, or in compelling me to openly oppose it to the destruction of my body…

During the interrogation, they said it was strange that I stood so strongly on conscience when I understood the concept so poorly. I replied that I was quite certain about my own diligently informed conscience, but did not choose to meddle with the conscience of others who disagreed with me.

It was also suggested that if I was really as willing to leave this world as to remain in it, I would speak out openly against the statute. My response was that I put no faith in my own goodness to ensure a happy afterlife, but looked rather to the love of God, and if He called me, I trusted in his great mercy to give me grace and strength.

Master Secretary said that he liked me less than before, when he had actually pitied me. Now, however, he had come to believe that my intentions were malicious.

Antony mourns Caesar, from *Julius Caesar* by Shakespeare

William Shakespeare (1560 – 1610) has left posterity a body of plays and poetry that have long astonished critics with the genius of their composition, their majestic command of the English language, and a profound understanding of human nature, politics, society and manners, history, and medicine, that defies belief. In the brief excerpt below, the Bard dramatizes the confrontation between Brutus, the most honourable of the conspirators who have just assassinated Caesar, and Mark Antony, the fallen dictator's heir. Brutus has rejected the warnings of Cassius and the other conspirators about allowing Antony to address the crowd, believing their cause to be just, and confident that he can convince the Roman populace to support them. Of course, he fails to take into account the eloquence of Antony, which turns public opinion against them. This encounter takes place immediately before the famous speech given by Antony to the Roman populace, a piece of rhetoric that modern politicians, businesspeople, and commentators could learn a great deal from.

CASSIUS

Brutus, a word with you.

(*Aside to Brutus*) You know not what you do; do not consent

That Antony speak in his funeral;
Know you how much the people may be mov'd
By that which he will utter?

BRUTUS
By your pardon;
I will myself into the pulpit first,
And show the reason of our Caesar's death;
What Antony shall speak, I will protest
He speaks by leave and by permission,
And that we are contented Caesar shall
Have all true rites and lawful ceremonies.
It shall advantage more than do us wrong.

CASSIUS
I know not what may fall; I like it not.

BRUTUS
Mark Antony, here, take you Caesar's body.
You shall not in your funeral speech blame us,
But speak all good you can devise of Caesar,
And say you do't by our permission;
Else shall you not have any hand at all
About his funeral: and you shall speak
In the same pulpit whereto I am going,
After my speech is ended.

ANTONY
Be it so.

I do desire no more.

BRUTUS

Prepare the body then, and follow us. (Exeunt all but ANTONY)

ANTONY

O, pardon me, thou bleeding piece of earth,
That I am meek and gentle with these butchers!
Thou art the ruins of the noblest man
That ever lived in the tide of times.
Woe to the hand that shed this costly blood!
Over thy wounds now do I prophesy,--
Which, like dumb mouths, do ope their ruby lips,
To beg the voice and utterance of my tongue--
A curse shall light upon the limbs of men;
Domestic fury and fierce civil strife
Shall cumber all the parts of Italy;
Blood and destruction shall be so in use
And dreadful objects so familiar
That mothers shall but smile when they behold
Their infants quarter'd with the hands of war;
All pity choked with custom of fell deeds:
And Caesar's spirit, ranging for revenge,
With Ate by his side come hot from hell,
Shall in these confines with a monarch's voice
Cry 'Havoc,' and let slip the dogs of war;
That this foul deed shall smell above the earth
With carrion men, groaning for burial.

Existential angst, from *Hamlet* by Shakespeare

William Shakespeare (1560 – 1610) created a veritable panorama of richly drawn characters who to this day invite new interpretation and analysis, underlining the profound psychological insights and understanding the Bard had at his command. Few people outside of academia are aware of the persistent controversy that has raged around this remarkable poet and story-teller, and it is a fact that his genius was not fully appreciated for a very long time. Scholarship has often been perplexed by his spontaneous mixing of the inspirational with the obscene, and tragedy with comedy. But his characters and the action are as multi-layered and unpredictable as life itself. Perhaps the most complex of all his characters is Hamlet, Prince of Denmark, caught up in a nightmarish situation in which his weak-willed mother has married his uncle, whom Hamlet suspects of the murder of his father, the king. The play explores the themes of existential uncertainty, the complexities of taking action, the haunting mystery of death, incestuous relationships, misogyny, and the sophistry that conceals and distorts truth, reducing human relationships to meaninglessness. Shakespeare sourced material for his plays from ancient and medieval histories, and he was a great admirer of Plutarch, the Greek historian and biographer. He may have taken the story of Hamlet from a twelfth-century history of Denmark compiled by Saxo Grammaticus or from the Histoires Tragiques by the French writer

*François de Belleforest. One word of advice – read the passage out loud,
as you should do with any piece of poetry or drama.*

HAMLET:

To be, or not to be: that is the question:

Whether 'tis nobler in the mind to suffer

The slings and arrows of outrageous fortune,

Or to take arms against a sea of troubles,

And by opposing end them? To die: to sleep;

No more; and by a sleep to say we end

The heart-ache and the thousand natural shocks

That flesh is heir to, 'tis a consummation

Devoutly to be wish'd. To die, to sleep;

To sleep: perchance to dream: ay, there's the rub;

For in that sleep of death what dreams may come

When we have shuffled off this mortal coil,

Must give us pause: there's the respect

That makes calamity of so long life;

For who would bear the whips and scorns of time,

The oppressor's wrong, the proud man's contumely,

The pangs of dispriz'd love, the law's delay,

The insolence of office and the spurns

That patient merit of the unworthy takes,

When he himself might his quietus make

With a bare bodkin? Who would these fardels bear,

To grunt and sweat under a weary life,

But that the dread of something after death,

The undiscover'd country from whose bourn

No traveller returns, puzzles the will

And makes us rather bear those ills we have
Than fly to others that we know not of?
Thus conscience does make cowards of us all;
And thus the native hue of resolution
Is sicklied o'er with the pale cast of thought,
And enterprises of great pith and moment
With this regard their currents turn away,
And lose the name of action. Soft you now!
The fair Ophelia! Nymph, in thy orisons
Be all my sins remember'd.

Laputa, from *Gulliver's Travels* by Jonathan Swift

Jonathan Swift (1667 –1745) is remembered and appreciated today as the author of the classic satire "Gulliver's Travels", but his literary legacy goes way beyond the merits of that undoubted masterpiece. An Anglo-Irish poet, satirist and political commentator, with a rare perspicacity and wit, Swift has always been controversial, and to this day, he provokes very mixed responses from readers and critics alike. This would hardly have troubled him very much because there is no doubt whatever that provocative is precisely what he set out to be when he put pen to paper. His description of the people of Laputa is an incisive piece of satire on the scientific community of his day.

These people are in a perpetual state of anxiety, incapable of enjoying a carefree moment. The turmoil in their minds is caused by matters that are trivial for other people. Their foreboding centres on changes they believe will occur in the planets and the stars.

For example, they worry that the Earth will eventually be swallowed up by the Sun, or that the surface of the Sun will become encrusted and heat and light for the Earth will be cut off. They are alarmed that the Earth was almost incinerated by the last close encounter with a comet, and they predict that the next one is scheduled to arrive in thirty-one years and will almost certainly annihilate us. They calculate that in its closest approach to the Sun it could absorb heat ten thousand times more intense than that of a red-hot poker, and would move away on its course with a fiery tail one million and fourteen miles in length. If the Earth happens to be swept by the tail around one hundred thousand miles from the comet itself, it would inevitably be set aflame and become in the process nothing but ash.

Moreover, they note that the Sun expends its energy daily without any means of replenishing its resources, and this means inescapable disaster for the Earth and the rest of the planets that depend on the heat and light from that star. So persistent are these fears and others like them for the people of Laputa that they are never able to sleep peacefully at night, nor even enjoy the ordinary pleasures and diversions of life.

The women of Laputa are spirited and fun-loving, and despise their husbands. They are also rather too interested in strangers, of whom there are many who visit the island from the continent below. These strangers are there on official business concerning their towns and corporations, or attending to personal matters, but Laputans treat them as inferiors because they are less prosperous.

However, the women take them as lovers. The trouble is that they behave in the most brazen manner because their husbands' minds are always totally consumed with other matters. The adulteress and her lover can indulge in the most intimate practices right under the husband's nose as long as he has his work to focus on, and doesn't have his Flapper to alert him to what is going on.

The wives and daughters of the Laputans resent the fact that they are supposed to remain on the island, even though it is the loveliest place in the world. They live in sumptuous luxury, and have the complete freedom of the island, but their passion is for the world outside and the attractions of the great city; and the only way they can feed that passion is with the permission of the king.

This is never readily granted for the simple reason that these people of position have learned through bitter experience that it is well nigh impossible to get the women to come back to Laputa.

It was made known to me that one aristocratic lady, the wife of the prime minister and mother of their many children, went down to Lagada, allegedly for health reasons. Despite the fact that her husband, who loves her very much in his own way, is one of the richest men in Laputa and has the finest mansion on the island, she remained absent for a lengthy period. Finally the king dispatched a group of men to bring her back, and she was discovered in a disreputable inn dressed in tatters.

She had sold all her fine clothes in order to fund the upkeep of a crippled servant who used to beat her frequently, and she angrily resisted being taken from him. She rejected her husband's generous forgiveness, and quickly absconded once more with all her expensive jewellery to rejoin her lover, never to be seen again.

The noble savage in *The Social Contract* by Rousseau

Jean Jacques Rousseau (1712 - 1778) was one of the most influential thinkers of the French Enlightenment and a leading instigator of the Romantic Movement, which extolled the idea of the innate goodness of man in his natural state, the myth of the noble savage, and the primacy of feelings over reason. It is in Rousseau that we see the seeds of the individual's quest for 'authenticity' in the nineteenth and twentieth centuries, and the revolt against bourgeois values. Rousseau himself lived a somewhat Bohemian lifestyle, and it is difficult to reconcile the sentiments of his writings with his personal treatment of other people, especially his own children. Nonetheless, as a writer Rousseau must be judged on his ideas and their impact. The French Revolution was certainly inspired in large part by him, and his impact on Kant and other modern thinkers was immense. To this day, he is quoted with approval in academia and other intellectual circles. This paraphrased passage from "The Social Contract" gives a thought-provoking introduction to his thinking, and demonstrates why so many people have for over two hundred years drawn inspiration from his ideas.

Let the reader find and follow the hidden, unremembered road travelled by man to get from the state of nature to the state of society. And if alongside the transitional stages I have just explained he painstakingly inserts all the others which time has not allowed me to include, or perhaps I have failed to identify, he will be above all amazed at how remote the two states are from one another.

By charting this gradual process he will be able to answer some of the questions of politics and ethics that continue to confound the philosophers. He will see that because people are different from age to age, Diogenes, who was looking for a type of man who had lived hundreds of years before, found nothing of the sort among his contemporaries. He will appreciate that the reason why Cato perished with Rome and the ideal of freedom was because he was at odds with the era in which he lived. Great men, who would have been accepted as rulers in another time, often serve only to bewilder their contemporaries.

In short, this explains how the soul and the emotions gradually change the very nature of man, and why our desires and gratification find new attachments. In this way, as a result of the natural man slowly but surely disappearing, society is now unable to produce anything more than counterfeit men and false emotions. These are the consequences of all those developments and none of them have any basis in nature itself.

Everything we can understand in this regard through rational thought is verified by observation. The emotional and affective gulf that divides the savage from civilised man is so great that what would make the one happy would render the other utterly despondent. The savage lives only for peace and freedom, wanting nothing more than to be left alone and to be free from having to work. Not even the tranquillity of the Stoic can equal the lack of concern the savage feels for artificial things.

By contrast, civilised man is never at rest, constantly working and driving himself to discover ever more burdensome responsibilities. He lives on the treadmill until his death, and risks destroying himself in order to live. He fawns before the powerful and the wealthy even though he hates them, and will do anything for the prestige of serving them. He feels no shame subjecting himself in his quest for security, and actually flaunts his chains and scorns those not fortunate enough to share them.

A Caribbean native would be dismayed by the farcical duties of a European minister of state, and would no doubt endure much suffering rather than live in that way. But of course, he could only have a proper appreciation of the European's lot if he understood the concepts of *power* and *reputation*.

He would have to understand that in society the opinions of others count for a great deal and that people value the judgments of others ahead of their own. In point of fact, the difference is that the savage finds his fulfilment within, while the civilised man lives like a parasite on the opinion of others.

There is no intention here to show the insensibility to good and evil that results from this, contradicting all our learned tomes on morality. Nor will I belabour the point that when perception trumps reality, the value of virtue is destroyed, and we even find ourselves boasting about our vices.

In truth, for all our humanity, philosophy, and civilisation, we present only a trivial and mendacious spectacle, esteem without virtue, rationality without wisdom, indulgence without fulfilment. All I needed to do was to show that this is not the natural state of man. It is the spirit of society and its inequality, and the corruption of our nature.

Executions, from *The Pursuit of Glory* by Tim Blanning

Tim Blanning (1942 -) is a professor of modern history at the University of Cambridge, a Fellow of the British Academy, and the author and editor of numerous books on European History. His book, "The Pursuit of Glory – Europe 1648 – 1815", is part of the Penguin History of Europe series, and covers the tumultuous period between the Treaty of Westphalia which ended the Thirty Years War and the fall of Napoleon in 1815. It is an engrossing survey of the great upheavals that ushered in the modern world – the scientific, industrial, American, French, and Romantic revolutions. The review below looks at Blanning's recounting of the two executions that proved to be watersheds in the political development of Britain and France.

Tim Blanning records how at 10.00am on Friday 17 January 1793 the outcome of a vote in the National Convention in France was publicised after more than thirty-six hours of debate. The resolution concerned the fate of Louis Capet, once Louis XVI, and more recently "King of the French".

The result was breathtakingly close, just a single vote among the 721 deputies tipping the scales in favour of the death penalty. The verdict was announced by Pierre Victurnien Vergniaud, the leading orator of the Girondin faction. "I declare in the name of the National Convention that the punishment it pronounces against Louis Capet is death."

The senior defence advocate, Chretien-Guillaume de Lamoignon de Malesherbes, relayed the bad tidings to the King, and Blanning notes that Louis would have known the outcome when his counsellor arrived in tears. Louis' words to Malesherbes are revealing: "I have been trying to think if, in the course of my reign, I did anything that deserved the slightest reproach from my subjects. Alas, M. de Malesherbes, I swear to you with all the sincerity of my heart, as a man who is about to appear before God, I have always wanted the happiness of the people."

Blanning points out that after more than three years of revolution, Louis still did not understand the nature of events in France. The "happiness of the people" was not the central issue.

Louis became emotional, first holding on to his advocate, and then walking distractedly around the room. Then he gathered his senses and tried to prepare for the ordeal ahead, dispatching a servant to the library of the Temple, the menacing fortress in which he had been imprisoned for the past six months. The book he sought was David Hume's "The History of England from the Invasion of Julius Caesar to the Revolution of 1688"

The words Louis wanted to read began: "Three days were allowed the king between his sentence and his execution. This interval he passed with great tranquillity, chiefly in reading and devotion."

The reference was obviously to Charles I of England, or "Charles Stuart", as he was referred to by the special court set up by the Commons of the Rump Parliament in January 1649. As it turned out, just 67 of the 135 commissioners were present at the session to resolve that "the said Charles Stuart, as a tyrant, traitor, murderer, and a public enemy, shall be put to death by the severing of his head from his body".

Charles' sentence followed a trial in which the King exhibited rather more integrity and flair than Louis was to display one hundred and fifty years later. The English king's adversaries erred by holding the trial at Westminster and arranging for the largest possible popular gallery. One of the most memorable moments in legal history occurred there when Charles outwitted his prosecutors without even uttering a word: on completion of the reading of the charges against him, the king burst out laughing and offered no further response.

Everything Charles did was orchestrated to undermine the authority of the court in the eyes of his subjects – he wore his high-crowned hat throughout the trial, and he thwarted attempts to have thirty-three special prosecution witnesses heard publicly by refusing to enter a plea.

Blanning tells how the rest of the trial produced more of the same, noting that even the most loyal of parliament's supporters had to admit that Charles ran rings around the presiding judge, John Bradshaw, and the chief prosecutor, John Cooke. Charles eloquently demonstrated that his opponents represented nowhere near a majority, that their popular support was a fiction, that the Lords opposed the trial, and that the trial was a violation of both Common Law and the Law of God.

A look into Burke's *Reflections on the Revolution*

Edmund Burke (1729 - 1797) was an Irish statesman, writer, and politician, who, after moving to England, served for many years in the House of Commons. As a Whig Conservative, the "Old Whigs", he provided moral support for the American colonies in their dispute with the government of George III, and then came out in strident opposition to the Revolution which broke out in France in 1789, as is demonstrated below. Burke's arguments give one a solid understanding of the very important distinction that has to be made between the European and British Enlightenments. His work provided the philosophical foundation of Anglo-American conservatism, and the excerpt below provides a brief insight into his thinking.

The consequences of the incompetence demonstrated by the so-called leaders of the people in France are supposed to be excused by saying that all was done in the name of liberty. Some do indeed take great liberty, but most of the people still suffer a humiliating repression. Does freedom have any meaning at all where there is no wisdom or virtue? It becomes the worst evil of all, issuing in foolishness, corruption, and licence, when there is no guidance or restraint.

People who understand the link between liberty and virtue hate to see the idea of freedom corrupted by irresponsible types with fine-sounding but hollow phrases. I have nothing against the uplifting emotions of freedom – they inspire us, they expand and unfetter our intellect, and they generate courage in times of danger. And even at my age I can be moved by the words of Lucan and Corneille. Nor am I totally opposed to the shallow diversions used to capture the popular imagination. They help people to understand important points, help to unite them, and also bring a bit of levity into mostly serious matters. Every politician needs to be broad-minded enough to embrace both custom and reason.

However, in momentous circumstances such as those in France, none of these trivialities are of any value.

Setting up a new government is not difficult: establish your authority, make people accept it, and that is that. And to provide liberty is even easier: simply let go of the reins. But to set up a free government, or in other words to reconcile the opposites of freedom and restraint in the state, is a much more demanding challenge. It requires a great deal of profound thinking from minds that are both wise and analytical. I cannot say I have seen anything like this from those who head the factions in the National Assembly in France.

It may well be that they are not as incompetent as they seem, but when politicians devote themselves to winning popularity, their abilities are worthless in framing a constitution. Instead of lawmakers they become sycophants; instead of conducting affairs they become mere instruments in the hands of the people. When one comes up with a plan for civic freedom that is rationally delineated and sensibly qualified, his rivals will respond with a plan of their own containing fewer restraints on the general populace. They will even question his loyalty to the cause of freedom.

The common people then begin to interpret moderation as a sell-out and compromise as treason. Ultimately, in trying to retain the influence that may enable him on occasion to water down some of the more extreme measures, a popular politician will be forced to establish powers that will sooner or later be fatal to any reasonable objectives he may have set.

It may be argued that there must surely be some things enacted by the National Assembly that are deserving of praise, and I have to concede that for all the violence and foolishness, there may be some good outcomes. If everything is destroyed, some bad things will inevitably disappear; and complete innovation is bound to produce some things that are good. Yet the question must be asked: might the good things have been achieved without resorting to violent revolution? And in truth the possibilities were there: every one of the new laws was in the process of consideration. Some old regulations have been rightly abolished, but they were mostly trivial matters that had no major impact on the general happiness.

The achievements of the National Assembly are slight; the mistakes they have made are serious.

Reign of Terror, in *Earthly Powers* by Michael Burleigh

Michael Burleigh (1948 –) is a widely respected and much published historian. His history of the Third Reich has been hailed as the finest ever, winning the Samuel Johnson Prize for non-fiction, and his work has been translated into fifteen languages. Burleigh has taught at Oxford, the London School of Economics, and Cardiff, and he has been a visiting professor at Rutgers, Washington and Lee, and Stanford universities. He is a member of the Academic Advisory Board of the Institut fur Zeitgeschichte in Munich and a Fellow of the Royal Historical Society. In this review of a short section from the first book of the outstanding two-volume set on politics and religion over the past two hundred years, "Earthly Powers" and "Sacred Causes", one gets a brief but graphic account of the horrors of the Jacobin Reign of Terror during the French Revolution. There are few more important books any leader in any field could read today.

Michael Burleigh records that with the coming of the Terror, the guillotine was used with such fury and fanaticism that the place of execution became a health hazard. Then the terrorists resorted to Ronsin's expedient of using artillery to mow down large groups of prisoners, leaving swordsmen to wander around slaughtering the wounded survivors. There were almost two thousand victims in Lyon by April 1794.

Fouche's New Year message to the Convention provided a template that would be used by Hitler, Stalin, and other mass murderers from then onwards:

"Our mission here is difficult and painful. Only an ardent love of country can console and reward the man who, renouncing all the affections which nature and gentle habits have made dear to his heart, surrendering his own sensibility and his own existence, thinks, acts, and lives only in the people and with the people, and shutting his eyes to everything about him, sees nothing but the Republic that will rise in posterity on the graves of conspirators and the broken swords of tyranny."

Burleigh points out that the revolt by moderate republicans in the provinces against the Jacobin coup had taken the pressure off the anti-revolutionary rebels in the Vendee region. However, once that threat was squashed, the Jacobins redirected their rage against the Vendeans. A recently defeated revolutionary army was redeployed to sweep the Vendee with chilling orders from the Committee of Public Safety:

"Kill the bandits instead of burning the farms, get the runaways and the cowards punished and totally crush this horrible Vendee...Plan with general Turreau the most assured means to exterminate all in this race of bandits."

The systematic state savagery which then reduced the Vendee to "a sad desert" was recorded in letters written by the perpetrators themselves. A captain in the Liberty battalion wrote to his sister:

"...wherever we pass by, we bring flames and death. Neither age nor sex are respected. Here, one of our detachments burns a village. A volunteer kills three women with his own hands. It's horrific but the health of the Republic is an urgent imperative. What a war! We haven't seen a single individual without shooting them. Everywhere is strewn with corpses; everywhere the flames bring their ravages."

Burleigh tells how Representative Jean-Baptiste Carrier took over the villa of a former slave trader where he cheated on his official mistress by cavorting with the local Nantais prostitutes. He used the guillotine for only the upper classes and the clergy, but to save ammunition when he needed to clear overcrowded prisons, he resorted to another evil ploy.

He would load groups of trussed prisoners onto barges which his men then sank in the middle of the River Loire. When prisoners managed to free themselves and tried to climb onto the boats sent out to bring back the crews of the sunken barges, drunken revolutionary soldiers would use their sabres to chop at the desperate hands. The comparison with what was to later happen in the many dictatorships of the twentieth century is obviously disturbing, to say the least.

Burleigh recounts that the sadistic treatment of their fellow human beings became a sport for many of the revolutionaries. For example, men and women were stripped naked, bound together in pairs, and drowned in what were referred to as "republican marriages". The atrocities wiped out a third of the people of the Vendee, a statistic comparable to the nightmare of Cambodia under the Khmer Rouge in the 1970s.

Guidance from George Washington's *Farewell Address*

George Washington (1732 – 1799) was born into to a family of Virginian planters, and given the education expected for a gentleman in colonial America. He served as a lieutenant-colonel in the Seven Years War between Britain and France, but, like his compatriots, he chafed under the constraints of British rule. On the outbreak of the American Revolution in 1775, he was appointed as Commander-in-Chief of the American forces, embarking on a six year struggle which ended with the British surrender at Yorktown. Washington could hardly be called a great general in the sense of an Alexander or a Napoleon, but he had the strength of character and a firm belief in the rightness of his cause to compensate for his deficiencies. A key figure in the drive for union and the new constitution, Washington was elected President unanimously by the Electoral College. He served two terms, but became disillusioned by the development of party politics, and this was reflected in his final address, a piece of which is paraphrased below.

I earlier indicated to you the severe threat posed by the development of political parties in the Republic, especially when they are established along geographical lines. It is now necessary that we look at the issue in more general terms, and I must at once sound a serious warning about the ruinous consequences of the whole ethos of party politics.

Regrettably, this ethos is of a piece with human nature, growing as it does from our most powerful emotions. It is present in different forms in all governments, regulated to some degree or other, but democracy unleashes its worst effects, and the spirit of party can become the gravest menace to a democratic state.

With rival parties taking turns in exercising the power of the state, usually animated by the vengefulness common in party conflict, men easily develop despotic attitudes. This has often been seen in other ages and nations where terrible atrocities have been committed. And, of course, in time this produces a more entrenched despotism.

The chaos and instability that come with party conflict soon persuade people to look for peace and security in the absolute power of one person, and the head of one of the contending parties seizes the opportunity to set himself up as dictator, riding roughshod over the rights of the people.

The spirit of party stirs up petty jealousies and bogus conflicts, incites various groups against each other, and sometimes provokes violent disorder in the streets. It also encourages foreign interference by opening ready access to the government through party channels.

Of course, there is the view that in a republic, party politics means that there are democratic constraints on government powers and that this helps to preserve liberty. To some extent this is certainly true, and in a constitutional monarchy party politics may be tolerated if not actively promoted. But where democratic institutions prevail, where governments are elected by popular majority, party politics are a danger.

Of the many predispositions that uphold political stability, religion and morality are the two essential pillars. Anyone who attempted to undermine these foundations of human happiness, these anchors of virtue and duty, would soon expose himself as an enemy of the people. Every politician, like every responsible citizen is bound to respect and nurture them. It would take many volumes to chart all their influence on private as well as public well-being. It is enough to consider where the security of property, reputation, and life would be without the religious obligation that makes the taking of oaths in courts of law meaningful and binding.

Moreover, the argument that morality can be upheld in society without the support of religion should be treated with the utmost suspicion. Whatever the merits may be of a proper education on the minds of the people, history and reason both make clear that national morality needs the religious principle.

It cannot be denied that virtue is an essential requirement of democratic government. In fact, this is true to a greater or lesser degree in the case of every form of free government. No one who sincerely supports the principle of popular democracy can remain inactive in the face of threats to its survival. That is why one of the top priorities must be to promote strongly the development of sound educational institutions, because the authority given to public opinion must be matched by popular enlightenment.

Lord Byron's maiden speech in the House of Lords

Alfred, Lord Byron (1788 – 1824) was one of the great Romantic poets, and is probably remembered by many as being "mad, bad, and dangerous to know", the description of him given by Lady Caroline Lamb, who was madly in love with him. But Byron was a complex character, whose life sheds valuable light on the era in which he lived, the age of revolution and reform, Napoleon and Metternich, and intense cultural ferment. Born with a deformed foot, he took pride in transcending the burden by participating in boxing, cricket, and swimming, and he once swam across the Hellespont. He was a voracious reader at Harrow and Cambridge, and his intellectual gifts ring out strongly from his poetry, his biting satire, and his speeches. He died of a fever at Missolonghi where he had gone to fight for Greek independence. The following is a paraphrase of his maiden speech in the House of Lords in 1812, in which he took up the cause of labourers who were breaking the machines that had taken away their employment.

Though I am a stranger to the House of Lords and to every person here whose attention I venture to ask for, I must claim a degree of your Lordships' indulgence by virtue of my connections with the county suffering these disturbances. I offer just a few observations on this issue, which I have to admit interests me deeply…

It is already common knowledge that every offence short of actual bloodshed has been committed, and that the owners of the machines that the rioters object to, as well as anyone thought to be connected with them, have been targets of abuse and violence. During my brief visit to Nottinghamshire just recently, scarcely a day passed when there was not some new outrage; and on the day I left the county, I was told that forty of the machines had been broken the night before. And again this was done without any resistance or disclosure…

However, while it is true that these offences are occurring at an alarming rate, it can hardly be denied that they have been sparked by conditions of unequalled suffering. The unrelenting determination of these wretched men in their activities suggests that nothing other than desperate need could have goaded a large group of people, once honest and hard-working, into committing crimes that put themselves, their families, and their community at such terrible risk…

You label these men as a mob, desperate, dangerous, and igno-rant, and you evidently believe that the only way to silence this many-headed beast is to cut off a few of its useless heads. How-ever, even a mob is more likely to listen to reason when treated in a firm yet conciliatory way, than it is when faced with increased penalties and added provocation. Are we aware of our obligation to the mob? It is they who work in your fields, serve in your homes, and fight in your army and navy, helping you while ne-glect and economic ruin have pushed them to the edge of despair. You call them a mob, but remember – a mob often speaks the feel-ings of the people…

I have travelled across the theatre of War in Spain, and I have visited some of the most oppressed provinces of the Ottoman Em-pire, but I have never witnessed such foul misery as I have seen since I returned to this Christian country. And what has been your response to all this? After months of hand-wringing, and actions worse than hand-wringing, you finally come up with your answer, the inevitable quack remedy offered by all state physicians since ancient times. You take the pulse of the patient, shaking your head sadly, and then prescribe the predictable remedy of warm water and bleeding – the warm water of your silly police and the scalpels of your soldiers – and announce that this terrible disorder will inevitably result in death, the inescapable outcome of the prescriptions of all political mountebanks...

Apart from the manifest injustice and the ineffectual nature of the Bill, are there not already enough provisions for capital punishment in your laws? Is there not enough blood on the books that more must be shed to testify against you in heaven? How will you administer this law? Can you imprison the entire county? Will you erect a gallows in every field and hang men like scarecrows?

A look at *Democracy in America* by Alexis de Tocqueville

Alexis de Tocqueville (1805 - 1859) was a French historian, social commentator, and politician who to this day continues to exert a strong influence on socio-political thought around the world. He entered politics after the 1830 Revolution in France as an opponent of the July Monarchy of Louis Philippe, and was active in the 1848 Revolution which toppled that regime. When the coup d'etat of Louis Napoleon was established, Tocqueville's opposition saw him arrested for high treason, but he was soon released, and retired from political life. Tocqueville's "Democracy in America" is a remarkable analysis of the great democratic experiment in the New World, and the insights remain well-worth reading and digesting for leaders in any field.

There comes a time in the life of a democratic society when the essential institutions are threatened from within. As the desire for material gratification gradually outstrips their education and their appreciation of their democratic institutions, people tend to lose their self-control in the face of exciting new possibilities. Totally absorbed in their desire to achieve prosperity, they easily forget the intimate relationship that exists between personal wealth and public well-being.

There is no need to resort to force against these people in order to deprive them of their freedoms. They unwittingly do the damage themselves. They regard the simple meeting of their political responsibilities as an obstacle that gets in the way of them pursuing their selfish interests. They believe that they never have the time to vote in elections, provide personal service to the popular government, or attend public meetings, and they refuse to waste their energies on these things. In fact, they regard them disdainfully as beneath men engaged in the real business of life. Ironically, they seem to imagine that they are standing on the principle of self-interest, but of course their understanding of that principle is very defective indeed: believing that they are devoting themselves to what they see as their own business, they disregard their first and most important business, that is, to preserve their liberty.

With the citizens now focused on their business rather than public affairs, and the leisured aristocracy a thing of the past, there is no one left to attend to the affairs of government. That presents an opportunity for any capable and ambitious man to seize control of the machinery of state, and he will encounter very little resistance. He merely has to nurture material progress in the country to satisfy the general population. Most importantly, he must maintain public safety and stability because men who are consumed by the desire for material gratification are more aware of the disturbances that freedom permits than they are of the fact that without freedom their enterprise would be impossible.

When the first hint of public unrest interrupts their business, they over-react, terrified as they are by the threat of anarchy. Indeed, they are ready to give up their freedom for a bogus security at the drop of a hat.

While I readily acknowledge that public safety is a great advantage, it is important to remember that nations have been enslaved by giving too much power to the government. This is not to say that people should hold peace and security in contempt, but they should want more out of life. A society that wants government to do no more than maintain order is already enslaved in its attitude to life; it is shackled by self-interest. In a society like that, the tyranny of party politics is as much to be feared as the dictatorship of an individual, because when most people are obsessed with private pursuits, even the most insignificant parties have an opportunity to prevail in public affairs. This is why we often witness in real life what we see on the stage at the theatre – a great mass of people represented by a handful of actors, who claim to speak in the name of the missing or distracted population.

Fortunately, up to this point in time the Americans have avoided all the pitfalls I have elucidated, and to this extent they fully deserve the respect of the rest of the world. There is probably no other country on earth that can boast as small a number of indolent people as America. Everyone who works shows a determination to improve their circumstances in life. But if the desire for material gratification is strong, at least it is guided, even if not fully controlled, by reason.

Resolve, from *The Second Inaugural* by Abraham Lincoln

Abraham Lincoln (1809 –1865) is generally acknowledged as the greatest of the presidents of the USA, and it seems fair to say that without his towering genius and remarkable strength of character in a social, political, and military crisis of staggering proportions, the United States would not have survived. A backwoodsman, provincial lawyer, and legislator, Lincoln proved to be an exceptional leader, building a "team of rivals" around him that, with his guidance and resolve, ensured victory and the preservation of the Union. His emancipation of the slaves was a turning point in the war and a watershed in American history. This excerpt from the speech given on the occasion of his Inauguration as President for a second term reflects the virtuous wisdom of the great champion of the Union.

Now, at the expiration of four years, during which public declarations have been constantly called forth on every point and phase of the great contest (the Civil War) which still absorbs the attention, and engrosses the energies of the nation, little that is new could be presented. The progress of our arms, upon which all else chiefly depends, is as well known to the public as to myself; and it is, I trust, reasonably satisfactory and encouraging to all. With high hope for the future, no prediction in regard to it is ventured.

On the same occasion four years ago, all thoughts were anxiously directed to an impending civil-war. All dreaded it -- all sought to avert it. While the inaugural address was being delivered from this place, devoted altogether to saving the Union without war, insurgent agents were in the city seeking to destroy it without war -- seeking to dissolve the Union, and divide effects, by negotiation. Both parties deprecated war; but one of them would make war rather than let the nation survive; and the other would accept war rather than let it perish. And the war came.

One eighth of the whole population were coloured slaves, not distributed generally over the Union, but localized in the Southern half part of it. These slaves constituted a peculiar and powerful interest. All knew that this interest was, somehow, the cause of the war. To strengthen, perpetuate, and extend this interest was the object for which the insurgents would rend the Union, even by war; while the government claimed no right to do more than to restrict the territorial enlargement of it.

Neither party expected for the war, the magnitude, or the duration, which it has already attained. Neither anticipated that the cause of the conflict might cease with, or even before, the conflict itself should cease. Each looked for an easier triumph, and a result less fundamental and astounding. Both read the same Bible, and pray to the same God; and each invokes His aid against the other. It may seem strange that any men should dare to ask a just God's assistance in wringing their bread from the sweat of other men's faces; but let us judge not that we be not judged.

The prayers of both could not be answered; that of neither has been answered fully. The Almighty has His own purposes. "Woe unto the world because of offences! For it must needs be that offences come; but woe to that man by whom the offence cometh!" If we shall suppose that American Slavery is one of those offences which, in the providence of God, must needs come, but which, having continued through His appointed time, He now wills to remove, and that He gives to both North and South, this terrible war, as the woe due to those by whom the offence came, shall we discern therein any departure from those divine attributes which the believers in a Living God always ascribe to Him? Fondly do we hope -- fervently do we pray -- that this mighty scourge of war may speedily pass away.

Yet, if God wills that it continue, until all the wealth piled by the bond-man's two hundred and fifty years of unrequited toil shall be sunk, and until every drop of blood drawn with the lash, shall be paid by another drawn with the sword, as was said three thousand years ago, so still it must be said "the judgments of the Lord, are true and righteous altogether"

With malice toward none; with charity for all; with firmness in the right, as God gives us to see the right, let us strive on to finish the work we are in; to bind up the nation's wounds; to care for him who shall have borne the battle, and for his widow, and his orphan -- to do all which may achieve and cherish a just, and a lasting peace, among ourselves, and with all nations.

Attacking the family in *The Communist Manifesto* by Marx

Karl Marx (1818 - 1883) was born in Trier, the son of a German Jew-ish lawyer. He was educated at the universities of Bonn and Berlin, but gave up the law for his interest in political philosophy. His meeting with Friedrich Engels in Paris led to their cooperation in setting up the Com-munist League for which they wrote "The Communist Manifesto" which laid the foundations for his later work "Das Kapital". Marx participated in the 1848 revolts and spent much of his life in exile in Britain, often living in extreme poverty. His ideas led to the communist totalitarian-isms of the 20th century, and his influence on language and modes of thought all round the world remains pervasive to this day. The paraph-rased excerpt laid out below is a reminder of the persuasiveness of Marx's rhetoric, but at the same time a clear exposition of the type of society he had in mind.

As Communists we advocate the destruction of the family; and even extremists are aghast at our call.

What is the foundation on which the bourgeois family is built? It is capital or private enrichment. This family is found in its most fully evolved form only among the bourgeoisie. But the rest of this picture of society is made up by the lack of family life among the labouring class, and in public prostitution.

When these other elements are swept away, the bourgeois family will disappear as well, and both will come to an end with the removal of capital.

Do you accuse us of desiring to bring an end to the selfish use and abuse of children by parents? We defiantly acknowledge the truth of the charge.

The objection is then immediately raised that we will bring down a sacred institution when we replace family education with social education.

What about your so-called family education – that too is social, driven by the established social mores and by the influence of society filtered through schools and other institutions? Communism is not the first to promote social values through education, but we unashamedly aim to change the nature of the intervention, and to liberate education from the control of the ruling class.

All this bourgeois nonsense about the family and education, extolling the virtues of the relationship between parent and child, has become horribly offensive. The heartless activities of modern industry have destroyed the bonds of the proletarian family, and the children are treated as chattels, mere items of commerce and industry to be exploited.

And so the protest erupts from the bourgeois ranks that the Communists would bring in the community of women. Bourgeois men consider their wives as means of production, and on hearing that the means of production are to be used in common, naturally conclude that women too will be shared.

They have no inkling that the actual intention is to ensure women are no longer regarded as a means of production.

In the final analysis, what could be more absurd than the self-righteous outrage of the bourgeoisie in contemplating the community of women, which they falsely assert to be the declared policy of the Communists? It is, of course, not necessary for us to initiate the community of women because it has been part of human society from the beginnings of civilisation.

It is not enough for our esteemed bourgeois to have ready access to the wives and daughters of the proletarians, not to mention the charms of prostitutes. They still delight in promiscuous behaviour with each others' wives.

The current practice of bourgeois marriage is actually no more than a way of having wives for communal use. That is why the most the Communists might reasonably be accused of is wanting to replace the deceitful existing system with an honest and legitimate community of women.

Beyond that, it should be plain enough that getting rid of the current system of production must logically entail demolishing the form of community of women that has grown out of that system. That means the abolition of prostitution, both public and private.

The totalitarian mindset, from *The Devils* by Dostoevsky

Fyodor Dostoevsky (1821 - 1881) was, together with Tolstoy, the greatest of the many Russian literary geniuses of the 19ᵗʰ and 20ᵗʰ centuries, and he remains one of the most influential figures in world literature to this day. Novels like "Crime and Punishment", "The Devils" (or "The Possessed"), "The Brothers Karamazov", and "The Idiot" reveal an understanding of human nature and the forces shaping the modern world few have equaled. I was once told by a well-known dissident Romanian intellectual that reading the four novels listed above, one after the other in quick succession, was a most effective way to give oneself a superb education. In this paraphrased excerpt from "The Devils", the anarchist Peter Verkhovensky and the murderous Stavrogin discuss the organization of their group of revolutionaries.

Peter Verkhovensky said: "What's the hurry?   We haven't formed even one group in this area yet."

"Then how did you manage to get all the leaflets distributed?" asked Stavrogin.

"Only four of the people at the meeting we are going to are members of the circle. The others are on trial and try to curry favour with me by spying on each other. They can be trusted, and we have to organise them before we move on. But I don't have to tell you, after all, you wrote the rules."

"Are you finding things difficult? Are there problems?"

"Problems? Things could hardly be better. Do you know what is really amusing? It's the effect official positions have on them. Few things motivate them more. That's why I invent all these positions – secretaries, undercover agents, bursars, supervisors, registrars, and the assistants – and they can't get enough of it. Then there's sentimentality – cheap emotion. It's the main driving force of socialism. But unfortunately, the people you appoint can let you down; even if you're careful you can still have problems. Then you can also get the complete scoundrels, who aren't too much of a challenge, and can sometimes actually be very useful, even if it does take a fair amount of one's time checking on them. Of course, the main factor in binding all these people together is their fear of thinking differently to the crowd – and what an advantage that is for us! They do anything to ensure they don't have to think for themselves – that would be terrible!"

"If that's the case, why go to all the trouble?"

"If someone's so readily available, you can't resist taking them in. Aren't you confident that we can succeed? You seem to have the faith, but lack the will. It's precisely people like these who ensure our success. They'll walk through fire for me. I only have to loudly accuse them of not being 'liberal' enough. There are fools who criticise me for deceiving people about the central committee and the network of branches; indeed, even you challenged me on that particular issue. But where's the deceit? You and I – we are the central committee. And there'll be as many branches as you may wish."

"More of the same sort of rabble?"

"Putty in our hands – they will be useful."

"So you still rely on me?"

"You're in charge. You have the drive. I'm just your subordinate. We'll board our ship, with its oars of maple, and sails of silk, and the beautiful Lisa at the helm…uh, what are the words of that old ballad?"

Stavrogin laughed loudly. "Are you stuck? Let me give your story a little energy. You talk about the forces at your disposal to motivate people – all that crowing about positions, and sentimentality being the cement that holds them together. I know an even more effective way. Simply induce four of the group to murder the fifth member on the pretext of his being a traitor, and you'll have them permanently bound together by the blood they have spilt. They'll be trapped and will never risk holding you responsible. Ha, ha, ha!"

Peter Verkhovensky remained silent, but reflected darkly on how Stavrogin would pay for those reckless words that very night.

A look at *Beyond Good and Evil* by Friedrich Nietzsche

Friedrich Nietzsche (1844 - 1900) was one of the most influential German Philosophers of the 19th century. Educated at the universities of Bonn and Leipzig, his brilliant intellect paved the way to an appointment as professor before he had even graduated. The influence he wielded from the start through works such as "Beyond Good and Evil" and "Thus Spake Zarathustra" grew rapidly and continues to this day, shaping the thinking of people both on the right and left of the socio-political spectrum. His ideas about the Superman, eternal recurrence, and the will to power, and his attack on Judeo-Christian morality sowed the seeds of nihilism and relativism, and provided encouragement for the totalitarian experiments and terrorism of the twentieth century. Nietzsche looked into the abyss of the dark side of human nature, and what he saw led him into the madness in which his mind was incarcerated for the eleven years leading to his death. The paraphrased excerpt below gives some indication of his worldview.

The current morality of Europe is a herd mentality, and it seems reasonable to suggest that it is only one of many different forms of morality, in particular higher moralities, that are possible.

For those of us who reject the current beliefs, and who see democracy as a degenerate political system that encourages mediocrity and weakness in man, we need to know who to look to for guidance. And our only alternative is new philosophers, original thinkers bold enough to propose different values, and to overturn allegedly "eternal values". We need pioneering spirits, leaders of the future who will now impose the constraints that will force succeeding generations to be innovative.

We have to teach humankind that the future is made by the human will. We must prepare for the massive and dangerous task of collective socialisation and education which is necessary if we are to end the shocking rule of foolishness and uncertainty known up to now as "history" – democracy is nothing more than its final manifestation.

The new philosophers and leaders we will need will completely overshadow all the religious, tyrannical, and benevolent authorities of the past. Is it legal for me to say it out loud, you free spirits, that the image of these new leaders is before our very eyes?

We know the conditions required to produce them; we know the probable ways and means of nurturing in a soul the high calling and drive to achieve the goals; we know that the transformation of values will demand a hard-hearted, unflinching resolve to carry the heavy responsibility; and we know the possibility that these new leaders may prove inadequate or fail or weaken. These are the things we worry about.

Nothing is so distressing as to have witnessed, predicted, or experienced the failure and decline of a great man. Yet the man who can see the possibility of humankind itself degenerating, he who, like us, understands the remarkably fortuitous development of humankind (a process untouched by the hand of God), he who perceives the destiny concealed beneath the silly imprudence and blind faith in "modern ideas", and even more so under the sway of Christo-European morality, that man suffers a mental torment like no other.

He knows intuitively that humankind could still be greatly improved by the coordination and development of human authority and institutions. He is completely convinced of the untapped potential, and he knows how many times in history humankind has stood at the crossroads. And he has painful memories of all the potentially up-lifting developments that have been shattered, wrecked, submerged, or made pathetic by unnecessary obstacles.

So what we see now is the general degeneration of humankind to the status of "the man of the future" – the pathetic ideal of socialist simpletons and superficial thinkers. This debasement and reduction of humankind to the level of completely social animals (or as is commonly claimed, to people of the "free society"), this degradation of man into a pygmy protected by equal rights and privileges, all this is without any doubt entirely possible.

Anyone who has considered this possibility and where it will lead, feels only contempt and a need to act.

A look at *Empire* by Niall Ferguson

Niall Ferguson (1964 -) is the Laurence A. Tisch Professor of History at Harvard, William Ziegler Professor of Business Administration at Harvard Business School, a Senior Research Fellow of Jesus College, Oxford University, and a Senior Fellow of the Hoover Institute at Stanford University. He is a stern critic of the European Union and authoritarianism in government, as has been seen with his denunciation of Vladimir Putin's policies in Russia. A controversial historian, no doubt, Ferguson still makes compelling reading, especially in the book "Empire: how Britain made the Modern World", in which he encourages a debate that still needs to be carried forward without prejudice and bigotry. This review of a short section from the book offers just a taste of the intellectual feast he provides.

Niall Ferguson acknowledges that there are many valid criticisms of the British Empire. Controversially, he dismisses the view of John Stuart Mill that British rule in India was "not only the purest in intention but one of the most beneficent in act ever known to mankind", and the opinion of Lord Curzon that "the British Empire is under Providence the greatest instrument for good that the world has seen".

He furthermore disputes the claim made by Jan Smuts, the Boer lawyer, commando, philosopher, and statesman that it was "the widest system of organised human freedom which has ever existed in human history". Ferguson, in fact, tries to pour cold water on the very notion that the British Empire was ever an altruistic institution in any manner or form.

He points out that the British were as determined in generating wealth through the slave trade in the eighteenth century as they were in later trying to eradicate slavery. In fact, British administrations were for a very long time guilty of the systematic racial discrimination and segregation that civilised people now deplore.

In the face of opposition to their control, British administrations often responded with ferocity, as in India in 1857, in Jamaica in 1831, in South Africa in 1899. Moreover, they were also exposed as callous in their reaction to famine, in Ireland in the 1840s, and in India in the 1870s. Moreover, it is not difficult to show that their attitude to other cultures was arrogant, to say the least.

However, as Ferguson goes on to assert, the British Empire made a greater contribution to the free movement of goods, capital, and labour than any other human organisation ever. It is also still unequalled as an agency for the spread of western standards of law, order, and governance across the globe.

Labelling these achievements as the fruits of "gentlemanly capitalism" seriously underestimates the many positive benefits that flowed from them. Similarly, to castigate the hierarchical nature of British colonial administration is to ignore the remarkable lack of corruption that characterised them. Millions of people came to enjoy the benefits of British Rule, which were essentially unknown in the colonies of the other European Powers.

Ferguson echoes the Shakespearean dictum that "The evil men do lives after them, the good is oft interred with their bones", and shows that the Empire was no exception. The trouble is, he says, that to try and imagine a world without the Empire is very difficult indeed. Playing that game with the French Revolution or the

First World War would be a possibility, but the Empire is less amenable to such intellectual wistfulness.

One is inclined to believe that it would all have happened anyway, just with different players. Another European power might have invented railroads and taken them around the world. Another might have introduced the telegraph in far-flung lands. Yet even when we concede that trade and commerce and migration would have proceeded as they always have, the dispersal of a distinctive culture and institutions still has to be explained. And it is here that benefits of the British Empire stand out.

Ferguson is right to emphasise that the coming of a British administration, or even just the extension of British influence in an area by means of military or financial pressure, brought with it certain unique aspects of British culture that offered at least the potential for all people to build a better future. He goes on to list the more important features:

1. The rich heritage of the English language; 2. English forms of land tenure; 3. Scottish and English banking practices; 4. The Common Law; 5. Various forms of Protestantism; 6. Team sports; 7. Limited government or the 'night watchman' state; 8. Representative legislative bodies; 9. The idea of freedom.

Looking at *The Ethics of Elfland* by G.K. Chesterton

Gilbert Keith Chesterton (1870 - 1936) was one of the greatest English writers of the nineteenth and twentieth centuries. His voluminous literary works included journalism, philosophy, poetry, biography, Christian apologetics, fantasy, and the famous Father Brown detective mysteries. Chesterton's distinctive combination of wit and wisdom always commanded a huge following and has ensured his enduring popularity. His political comments often displayed his love of paradox as well as his serious socio-political concerns: "The whole modern world has divided itself into Conservatives and Progressives. The business of Progressives is to go on making mistakes. The business of the Conservatives is to prevent the mistakes from being corrected." The following piece is a paraphrased excerpt from one of his best-loved essays. It seems wildly ambitious to paraphrase Chesterton, but here goes...

From first to last, the philosophy I have believed with uninterrupted confidence is that which I learned in the nursery. For the most part, I learned it from a nurse, that high-minded priestess of democracy and tradition.

The things I believed in most firmly in those early days, and as I still do now, are the things called fairy tales. These always seem to me to be the completely reasonable ideas and beliefs of human-kind.

They are not fantasies; alongside them, everything else is fantastic. Placed next to fairy tales, both religion and rationalism are strange, though religion is strangely right and rationalism is strangely wrong. The realm of fairy tales is nothing more than the bright land of common sense.

But I am concerned here with the morality and philosophy that come from fairy tales. In a more comprehensive description I could list many virtues that flow from them. Take the lesson in chivalry from *Jack the Giant Killer* that tells us that giants ought to be killed for the very reason that they are gigantic. It is an honourable rebellion against pride. For the rebel has been around longer than all the kingdoms, and opposing tyranny has more tradition than fighting for kings.

The lesson of *Cinderella* echoes that of the Magnificat – honour the virtue of humility. *Beauty and the Beast* teaches us that it is in loving someone that we make them loveable. And the ominous parable of *Sleeping Beauty* recalls how humans were blessed with all manner of gifts, yet tormented by death, and also how death may be assuaged to become merely a sleep.

However, I am not focusing on the different laws of Elfland, but rather the entire ethos behind it, which I took in before I could speak, and will hold long after I cease to write. I am talking about a particular way of viewing life, which was nurtured in me by the fairy tales, but which has ever since been confirmed by the facts.

Let me put it this way. There are progressions or developments in life where one thing ensues from another, which are, in line with the proper meaning of the word, reasonable. And they are, in line with the proper meaning of the word, necessary. These progressions are simply mathematical and logical.

In Elfland, we are the most reasonable of all creatures, and we accept that reason and that necessity. For example, the fact that

159

the Ugly Sisters are older than Cinderella makes it necessary that Cinderella is younger than them...Since Jack is a miller's son, then a miller must be his father. Impartial reason commands it from her intimidating throne, and we in Elfland dutifully comply. When the three brothers are mounted on three horses, you have six animals and eighteen legs in action. That is rationalism in its proper sense, and it is recognised in Elfland.

However, looking over the hedge of Elfland at the natural world, I saw a strange spectacle – academics in glasses discussing real things, like dawn and death, as though *those things* were rational and necessary. They were saying that the fact that trees produce fruit was as necessary as the fact that one tree plus two trees equals three trees. Of course, that is not the case.

The test of Elfland shows there is a huge difference; and the test is the imagination.

It is not possible to imagine one plus two not adding up to three. But it is possible to imagine trees not producing fruit; you can imagine candlesticks on the branches, or tigers suspended by their tails...

In Elfland we have always recognised a clear difference between the science of mental relations, where there are indeed laws, and the science of physical facts, where there are no laws, just strange repetitions. We believe in physical miracles, but not mental impossibilities. We believe that a beanstalk grew all the way up to another world in the sky, but remain perfectly clear about the number of beans that make five.

A courtroom defence of integrity by Mohandas Gandhi

*Mohandas Karamchand Gandhi (1869 – 1948) was the most promi-
nent political and spiritual leader in India in the decades leading up to
independence. He was brought up in the Jain tradition, believing in
compassion for sentient beings, vegetarianism, fasting for personal puri-
fication, and tolerance between all creeds. After studying law at University College London, he landed up in Natal, South Africa, where he experienced the racism rife in almost all quarters of the country. His experiences in the Boer War and the Bambatha Rebellion, led him to feel
deep repulsion at the ugly treatment of his fellow human beings. Returning to India in 1915, Gandhi became active in the resistance to British rule, urging non-violent resistance through civil disobedience. A
stern opponent of partition, Gandhi worked hard to reconcile Hindu and
Muslim factions, and he was disappointed with the settlement ultimately
reached. He was assassinated by a Hindu extremist in 1948. The excerpt
below rings out with the greatness of Gandhi and his remarkable contribution to human civilisation.*

Before I read this statement I would like to state that I entirely
endorse the learned Advocate-General's remarks in connection
with my humble self. I think that he was entirely fair to me in all
the statements that he has made, because it is very true and I have
no desire whatsoever to conceal from this court the fact that to

preach disaffection towards the existing system of Government has become almost a passion with me, and the Advocate-General is entirely in the right when he says that my preaching of disaffection did not commence with my connection with Young India but that it commenced much earlier; and in the statement that I am about to read, it will be my painful duty to admit before this court that it commenced much earlier than the period stated by the Advocate-General. It is a painful duty with me but I have to discharge that duty knowing the responsibility that rests upon my shoulders, and I wish to endorse all the blame that the learned Advocate-General has thrown on my shoulders in connection with the Bombay occurrences, Madras occurrences and the Chauri Chaura occurrences.

Thinking over these things deeply and sleeping over them night after night, it is impossible for me to dissociate myself from the diabolical crimes of Chauri Chaura or the mad outrages of Bombay. He is quite right when he says, that as a man of responsibility, a man having received a fair share of education, having had a fair share of experience of this world, I should have known the consequences of every one of my acts. I know them. I knew that I was playing with fire. I ran the risk and if I was set free I would still do the same. I have felt it this morning that I would have failed in my duty, if I did not say what I said here just now.

I wanted to avoid violence. Non-violence is the first article of my faith. It is also the last article of my creed. But I had to make my choice. I had either to submit to a system which I considered had done an irreparable harm to my country, or incur the risk of the mad fury of my people bursting forth when they understood the truth from my lips. I know that my people have sometimes gone mad. I am deeply sorry for it and I am, therefore, here to submit not to a light penalty but to the highest penalty. I do not ask for mercy. I do not plead any extenuating act...

In fact, I believe that I have rendered a service to India and England by showing in non-co-operation the way out of the unnatural state in which both are living. In my opinion, non-co-operation with evil is as much a duty as is co-operation with good. But in the past, non-co-operation has been deliberately expressed in violence to the evil-doer. I am endeavouring to show to my countrymen that violent non-co-operation only multiplies evil, and that as evil can only be sustained by violence, withdrawal of support of evil requires complete abstention from violence.

Non-violence implies voluntary submission to the penalty for non-co-operation with evil. I am here, therefore, to invite and submit cheerfully to the highest penalty that can be inflicted upon me for what in law is a deliberate crime, and what appears to me to be the highest duty of a citizen. The only course open to you, the Judge and the assessors, is either to resign your posts and thus dissociate yourselves from evil, if you feel that the law you are called upon to administer is an evil, and that in reality I am innocent, or to inflict on me the severest penalty, if you believe that the system and the law you are assisting to administer are good for the people of this country, and that my activity is, therefore, injurious to the common weal.

Contemplating *The Servile State* by Hilaire Belloc

Hilaire Belloc (1870 - 1953) was born in France, but educated for the most part in Britain, and he became a naturalised British subject in 1902. He initially dabbled in politics, but gave up his political career to devote himself to writing. Belloc became a historian, poet, and essayist of note, and his general knowledge and energetic lifestyle astonished all who came to know him. Lady Diana Cooper said of him that he was "with Winston Churchill the man nearest to genius I have known, one of the most complex, contradictory, and brilliant characters ever to rumble, flash and explode across this astonishing world of ours. He was the 'Captain Good' in life as well as the minstrel, the story teller, the soothsayer, the foundation and the flush of the feast." Belloc was the close friend of G. K. Chesterton, and the two men became active proponents of the socio-economic theory of Distributism. The paraphrased excerpt below is from his classic and controversial book, "The Servile State", and it shows Belloc's remarkably prescient understanding of the seemingly intractable challenges that have come to haunt our modern socio-political arrangements.

If you try to eradicate the evils of capitalism by fixing the one of its two aspects which is revealed as the unjust distribution of property, there are only two options open to you.

If there is widespread suffering as a result of property being in the hands of too few people, you can change things either by giving possession of property to many or by giving possession of property to none. There is no third way open to you.

Giving possession of property to no one means, in effect, entrusting the stewardship of all property to government officials. If you believe the evils that flow from capitalism arise because of the institution of property itself and not the rapacity of the few, then you must prohibit private citizens in the community from owning any of the means of production. But, of course, the means of production have to be in the hands of someone, or we would all be without food, clothing, and housing. That is why, effectively, this idea comes down to the control of the means of production by public officials.

From an economic point of view, this expedient does not depend in any way upon whether those officials are controlled by the public or not. The fundamental fact to be noted is that there is in this matter a simple choice: private property or public property. Somebody must organise for the ploughing to be done, and must control the ploughs, or else there will be no ploughing carried out at all.

In the same way, it is perfectly clear that if you believe that property per se is not evil, but rather the fact that it is in so few hands, then you must somehow see that ownership is given to many more people.

In the light of these realities, we may sum up by noting that a society like our own, averse to the idea of slavery, and opposed to any deliberate revival of the institution of slavery, is of necessity obliged to consider the reform of its property laws on one of two systems. One is the dismantling of private property and the setting up of the system known as collectivism, which puts the control of the means of production in the community in the hands of public officials. The other is the distribution of property on an increasing wide scale until the entire state is characterised by the system, and all free citizens are as a matter of course owners of land or capital or both.

The first of the two systems constitutes a socialist or collectivist state; the second constitutes a proprietary or distributive state.

Having clarified these points, I will in the next section go on to demonstrate why the latter system, which entails the redistribution of property, is dismissed as unachievable by our capitalist society, and why, as a result, reformers tend to come out in support of the socialist or collectivist model.

Thereafter, I will go on to explain how from the very outset all socialist reform is unavoidably diverted and becomes something completely different from what it was meant to be. It evolves into a society in which there are still very few owners and the labouring classes sacrifice their freedom for security. The capitalist system breeds a socialist or collectivist mindset which in turn gives rise to something totally different from socialism: it produces the servile state.

The Unity of Philosophical Experience
by Etienne Gilson

Etienne Gilson (1884 – 1978) was a French philosopher and historian who was largely instrumental in the revival of medieval studies that occurred in Europe and America after the First World War. A Professor at the Sorbonne in Paris, he also became a popular visiting lecturer at Harvard University at the same time as luminaries such as Alfred North Whitehead. He was invited to give the William James Lectures in 1936 on the occasion of Harvard's 300th anniversary. His lectures were then published as the book "The Unity of Philosophical Experience". This brief review of a section from that book gives some indication of the remarkable understanding of the history and nature of the philosophical endeavours of humankind available to the more curious reader.

Etienne Gilson emphasises that only philosophy can explain the history of philosophy. This being the case, the historical fact that specific philosophical standpoints recur again and again through the ages should alert observers to the possibility of some metaphysical necessity.

He points out that the most salient recurrence involves the renewed philosophical investigations that are sparked by every crisis of scepticism. Gilson says that because this recurring reality impacts on the very life of philosophy itself, it is not merely remarkable, but must be the most basic truth of all. And if such a metaphysical necessity exists, what is it?

Gilson then demonstrates the historical reality of the recurrence. The starting point is the idealism of Plato, which prompts Aristotle to warn that it would result in scepticism. Then Greek scepticism proves that Aristotle's fears were entirely warranted, but the scepticism is eased by the moralism of the Stoics and the Epicureans, and the mysticism of Plotinus. Confidence in mankind's ability to know reality is restored by St. Thomas Aquinas, but soon after, William of Ockham strikes at the very roots of the new understanding, initiating the scepticism of the late Middle Ages and the Renaissance. This in turn is countered by the moralism of the Humanists and the pseudo-mysticism of Nicholas of Cusa and his followers.

Descartes and Locke precipitate a new attack on human knowledge leading to the scepticism of Berkeley and Hume, which then provokes the moralism of Rousseau and the visions of Swedenborg. Kant was influenced one way or another by Rousseau, Swedenborg, and Hume, but his attempt to build a secure foundation for philosophical knowledge promoted a variety of modern agnostic mindsets and a welter of moralistic creeds and pseudo-mysticisms for those driven to spiritual despair. It seems the alleged death of philosophy is consistently accompanied by its revitalisation, and that would suggest another new authority is close at hand. Gilson maintains that the first law of philosophical experience is: *Philosophy always buries its undertakers.*

Sceptics will argue that it is scepticism that keeps recurring, and though opponents of philosophy tend to be unphilosophical, philosophy itself is obliged to respond with intellectual honesty. This was why Kant, in declaring all metaphysical knowledge to be an illusion, still looked for the source of that illusion in the essence of reason itself. Hume's scepticism had attacked both metaphysics and science, and Kant tried to save science by sacrificing meta-

168

physics. Gilson contends that Kant's experiment only demonstrated that if metaphysical knowledge is arbitrary, then so is scientific knowledge, and the conclusion is inescapable: our conviction that science provides objective validity is tied to our belief in the objective validity of metaphysics. The question is not "Why is metaphysics a necessary illusion?" but "Why is metaphysics necessary?" And it must further be asked why it is that metaphysics has given rise to so many illusions.

All metaphysical systems, that is, all philosophies, agree on the necessary goal of finding the first cause of everything that exists. Democritus called it matter; Plato the Good; Aristotle the self-thinking Thought; Plotinus the One; Christian philosophers said it was Being; Kant saw it as the Moral Law; Schopenhauer the Will; Hegel the absolute Idea; Bergson the Creative Duration; and there are many others.

Gilson asserts that in every case, the philosopher is a person who seeks behind and beyond experience for an ultimate source of all of reality. He points to the objective fact that this quest has gone on for more than twenty-five centuries, and that after concluding it was a waste of time and vowing never to search for it again, man has always returned to the quest. This law of the human mind is at least as certain as any empirically proven law.

A look at *Homage to Catalonia* by George Orwell

George Orwell (1903 - 1950) was born Eric Arthur Blair, the son of a colonial civil servant in India. He was educated at Eton and after a stint in the Indian Imperial Police in Burma, he decided to become a writer. After hard times in Paris and London, he achieved success under his new name, and his first book was published in 1933. Initially an anarchist, Orwell later became a socialist, and he joined the republican forces in Spain in 1936 to fight against Franco. His experiences in Spain, where the Communists tried hard to destroy their revolutionary socialist allies, made him a passionate opponent of Stalinism, and his best-known novels, "Animal Farm", and "1984", grew out of this mind-set. Certainly one of the greatest English essayists of the twentieth century, Orwell continues to exert influence all over the world both as a prose writer of rare ability and as an eloquent adversary of totalitarian ideals. The following paraphrase of an excerpt from his book, "Homage to Catalonia", shows why Orwell will never lose his relevance.

Superficially, it appeared as if the Communists and the POUM (Partido Obrero de Unificacion Marxista – a dissident anti-Stalinist group) disagreed about tactics. The POUM wanted to sweep aside the old order without delay, while the Communists were more measured, and both sides had plausible arguments. But the Communists also alleged that the unity of the government forces was undermined by POUM propaganda, and that this undermined the war effort. Even though I would dispute their claim, it was a reasonable point they made.

This is where one could discern the real character of the Communist approach. Initially reasonable, they became increasingly fractious and vociferous thereafter. They said that the POUM were creating divisions in the government ranks not merely through poor judgment but rather as a deliberate strategy. Labelling the POUM as Fascists incognito, who were secretly supporting Franco and Hitler, they claimed there was a plot to launch a bogus revolution as a precursor to a Fascist coup. They called the followers of the POUM "Trotskyites" and members of "Franco's Fifth Column".

It was absurd to lay a charge of treason against many thousands of working class people, including almost ten thousand soldiers who were dug in on the front-line in freezing conditions, not to mention the hundreds of people from other countries who had given up careers and their passports to make a stand against Fascism in Spain. Yet this is precisely what they did on posters and leaflets which were distributed throughout the country, and also in the tendentious Communist media all over the globe. Examples were copious.

And so we were called Trotskyites, Fascists, traitors, murderers, cowards, secret agents, and so on. It left a bad taste in the mouth when one recalled the actual type of people who were involved in our struggle. It is disheartening to watch a teenage Spanish boy, his face white with shock, stretchered to the rear, all the while knowing personally the fashionable people in London and Paris who are at that moment churning out propaganda accusing the boy of being a Fascist and a traitor.

The propaganda is among the worst aspects of war, and the shrill deceitfulness and hate is raised by people far away from the danger. In the front-line, I was never once called a Trotskyite or a renegade by any of the Communist soldiers in the PSUC or the International Brigade; it was the journalists at the rear who did the real damage. We were reviled by people who got no closer to the action than the newspaper offices in Valencia. All the bluff and bravado came, as always, from people who had no first-hand experience of the fighting, and who would have fled in horror at the thought of taking up arms.

It has been depressing to learn the truth about the Left-wing media, who are fully the equal of those on the Right when it comes to specious and deceitful reporting. I still sincerely believe that those of us on the government side fought in this conflict for motives far more worthy than those of imperialist campaigns, but the propaganda distorted the picture. The barrage of abuse from both Left and Right was a feature of the war from the beginning. The Daily Mail screamed: "REDS CRUCIFY NUNS", while the Daily Worker insisted that Franco's Foreign Legion was made up of murderers, white slavers, dope-addicts, and trash.

A look at Hannah Arendt's *Eichmann in Jerusalem*

Hannah Arendt (1906 - 1975) was a German Jew, born in Hanover. She received her doctorate in philosophy at the University of Heidelberg, having studied under the eminent philosophers Karl Jaspers and Martin Heidegger. She had an affair with the latter. In 1933 she was arrested briefly by the Gestapo, and thereafter fled to Paris where she worked for Jewish organizations helping to get refugees to the Middle East. In 1940 she went to the United States, and became a citizen ten years later. Despite her many controversial views, Arendt remains an important writer for posterity, rich in personal insight into the workings of the totalitarian mindset. The following paraphrase of an excerpt from her reflections on the Nazi, Adolf Eichmann, conveys some of the power of her theme and her insights

Himmler was the most talented of the Nazi leaders when it came to easing a troubled conscience. He was the author of motivational slogans like that of the S.S. first used by Hitler in 1931: "My honour is my loyalty". Eichmann described them as "winged words" but the judges at Nuremburg sharply dismissed them as "empty talk". According to Eichmann, Himmler bestowed them at the end of each year, perhaps together with a nice Christmas bonus.

The only one that Eichmann recalled was one he used time and again: "Future generations will not be required to fight these battles again." Of course, the line referred to the battles of conscience when the Nazis brutalised women, children, the aged, and other vulnerable people.

Among the other lines of self-justification used by Himmler in addressing the officers of the Einsatzgruppen commanders, the S.S. elite, and Police commanders, we find: "To have persevered and, aside from the inevitable exceptions arising from human frailty, to have stayed pure, that has steeled us to the task. This glorious episode in our history has never been written and never will be." Or: "The command to resolve the issue of the Jews was the most terrifying any institution could ever be given." Or: "We know that what we demand of you is 'super-human', that is, to be inhuman in a super-human way."

As it happened, all their expectations were met. But it is remarkable that Himmler seldom resorted to ideology to justify the barbarism. What motivated these murderers was the idea that they were part of a momentous historical event – "a noble task that occurs only once in two millennia" – which logically would be a strenuous challenge. But note that these men were not born sadists or murderers; in fact, there was actually a methodical campaign on the part of the Nazi bosses to remove any functionaries who seemed to enjoy the terrible work.

The Einsatzgruppen recruited from the Armed S.S., a unit in no way exceptional in terms of cruelty, and Heydrich picked the officers from the S.S. elite who were all university educated. The challenge was not to defuse their conscience but rather the natural pity all normal human beings feel in the face of physical suffering. Himmler himself was squeamish and the ploy he used to overcome his own feelings was applied to the men – it involved redirecting the pity towards oneself. Rather than thinking of the "terrible pain I inflicted on others", the murderers were encouraged to focus on the "terrible suffering I had to bear as a matter of duty." What a monstrous burden!

The year 1939 saw the first gas chambers built in response to Hitler's decree that "terminally ill people should be granted the right to mercy killing". This probably explains the hideous belief of Dr. Servatius that death by gas should be purely a medical matter. It was not a new idea.

Several years before, in 1935, Hitler had informed his Reich Medical Head, Gerhard Wagner, that war would make it easier for him to carry out his plans for euthanasia. The decree was given immediate effect in regard to the mentally ill, and between December 1939 and August 1941 some fifty thousand citizens were gassed in facilities in which the death chambers were made to look like showers and bathrooms in much the same way as they were at Auschwitz thereafter…

Of all the state-directed language guidelines which were deliberately deployed to mislead people and confuse the issues, the most powerful influence on the minds of the killers came from Hitler's first decree, which allowed and encouraged murder to be justified as mercy killing.

Betrayal, in *Man's Search for Meaning* by Viktor Frankl

Viktor Frankl (1905 – 1997) was an Austrian neurologist and psychiatrist. His experiences as an inmate in the Nazi death camps at Auschwitz and Dachau naturally impacted dramatically on his ideas as a psychiatrist, and in the years after the war he became one of the leading doctors in his field. He developed the method called logotherapy, a form of existential analysis, known as the Third Viennese School of psychotherapy. His best-selling book, "Man's search for meaning" is a riveting first-hand account of life in the concentration camps. It makes it impossible for anyone who reads it to ignore the great existential questions raised by that gruesome and disturbing chapter in the history of civilisation. This paraphrase of an excerpt from the book provides a glimpse into the devastating reflections of a doctor who was also a victim in one of the most revealing episodes of the story of humanity.

This account of life in the camps is not about the courage and sacrifices of famous people, and it is not about the more prominent among the Capos, that is, the prisoners who were put in positions of authority and given special privileges. Rather than focussing on the challenges faced by the people in charge, it focuses on the agonies and deaths of the immense multitude of anonymous innocents who became victims of the Nazis.

The Capos showed utter disdain for these ordinary inmates who had no rank to distinguish them. While these despised people had to try and survive on starvation rations, the Capos always had as much to eat as they wanted. If truth be told, many Capos had probably never had it better in their lives. And their treatment of the other prisoners was frequently more vicious than that of the guards themselves, and the physical abuse they were guilty of was much worse than that perpetrated by the S.S.

Of course, the Germans specifically appointed as Capos men of a weak or sadistic nature, and if they failed to do the evil work expected of them, they were quickly returned to the main body of prisoners. Those who performed as the Germans wanted them to soon demonstrated a psychology comparable to that of the S.S. men and the wardens.

Apathy was among the more common mindsets the prisoners exhibited, and it went beyond a simple defensive response to the terrible situation in which they found themselves. It indubitably arose from grossly inadequate food and sleep, and also from the volatility of the general mood among them, and the fact that prisoners were denied tobacco and coffee. Sleep deprivation was the inevitable consequence of severe overcrowding, the appalling absence of hygiene and sanitation, and the entirely predictable infestation by vermin.

There were, of course, also many other psychological factors to take into consideration. Most of the prisoners were weighed down by a type of inferiority complex. To have thought of ourselves for as long as we could remember as possessing personal dignity and being worthy of respect, and to suddenly have that wrenched away from us, made us feel that our very identities had been destroyed.

Of course, the consciousness of human dignity is a spiritual quality unassailable by physical hardship in people of faith and strong character, but even free people often lack it. That the prisoners felt debased was completely understandable.

It was easy enough to study this development simply by noting the radical differences in the sociological dispositions on display in the camp. Those prisoners whose status had been elevated – the Capos, the cooks, the store-men, and policemen – for the most part experienced no sense of degradation at all. In fact, they regarded them selves as superior, with some even manifesting petty delusions of grandeur.

The attitude adopted by the greater mass of deprived and despised prisoners to this privileged elite drawn out of their ranks was predictably damning, often giving rise to sardonic humour. For example, one prisoner was heard telling a companion about the background of one of the Capos: "Just to think – I can remember when that man was only the president of a leading bank. Fortune must have smiled on him to help him rise to such a prominent position in life."

The potential for conflict between the prisoners and their "elite" brethren was enormous, especially when it came to the distribution of food. Not surprisingly, violent brawls often erupted in the camp at mealtimes.

The experiences of internment prove that man never loses his freedom to choose what he will do. There were many examples of men who conquered their apathy and anger, even in the most brutal conditions imaginable. The human spirit can always transcend the circumstances of life, overcoming the torments of extreme psychological and physical duress.

A look at *The Road to Serfdom* by Friedrich Hayek

Friedrich Hayek (1899 - 1992) was an Austrian economist. He made his name as one of the pioneers of monetary theory and in 1974 became co-winner of the Nobel Memorial Prize in Economics. He is also regarded as one of the leading advocates for libertarianism in the twentieth century. Hayek's magnum opus, "The Road to Serfdom", started out as a memo, became a magazine article, and was eventually expanded into a book. Often misrepresented by ideologues on the left and the right, the book is a reflection on the dynamics of personal liberty and government authority. As is always the case, it is better to read the original than to listen to the critics pushing their own ideological agendas. This paraphrase of a passage from the book echoes the warnings of Orwell, Guardini, Solzhenitsyn, and many others.

The most efficient method of persuading people to affirm the soundness of a set of values is to convince them that they are in fact the very ones that good people have always embraced, even though they have not always been clearly understood and fully appreciated. This involves inducing people to shift their commitment from the old loyalties to new ones on the pretext that the latter conform to people's better instincts, even if it has taken time for proper understanding to emerge.

This objective is best achieved by keeping the old words but changing the meaning. The wholesale corruption of language is a central feature of the intellectual milieu of totalitarian states, yet uninformed people continue to be hoodwinked by it. They fail to take account of the new meanings attached to familiar terms.

The most egregious example must surely be the word "liberty". This term is as commonly and as loosely bandied about in authoritarian states as anywhere else. Admonitions aplenty have alerted us to the danger of charlatans who urge us to trade our old liberties for the new ones, and wherever freedom properly understood has been dismantled, you will find the justification has been the introduction of some "new liberty" vouchsafed to the people.

Ominously, even in the West there are social engineers who propose a new collective freedom. It is disturbing that its champion feels compelled to reassure the public that "planned freedom" does not necessarily mean the demise of all established liberties. It gets worse when he takes care to point out that the understanding of freedom that has come down from preceding generations tends to confuse the issue.

In reality, he perverts the meaning of the word "freedom" as completely as do the totalitarian bosses. Like them, he has no interest in the freedom of the individual, but only in the unimpeded liberty of the social engineer to mould society according to the ideological vision. Using the word "freedom" to try and justify placing unlimited power in the hands of state officials is blatant cynicism and the height of perversity.

Of course, a distinguished line of German thinkers and socialist ideologues has paved the way for the corruption of the meaning of "freedom". But there are many other important words whose meanings have literally been turned inside out with a view to serving totalitarian interests. Consider only the important concepts of justice, law, right, and equality. And it doesn't end there; the meanings of all ethical and political words are now at risk.

Unless a person is actively alert to the on-going campaign, it becomes increasingly hard to apprehend the enormous extent of this transformation of language, the consequent confusion, and the impossibility of rational discourse. One needs to actually see what happens when one of two brothers adopts the totalitarian vision, and within a short time is no longer capable of communicating effectively with his sibling.

The fact that the manipulation of words is an on-going process as opposed to a single campaign makes the whole matter much more insidious. Gradually, the process will destroy the language, leaving words as empty shells and meaning as a matter of personal whim.

As has been demonstrated in this century, it is no great challenge for a totalitarian government to destroy independent thinking in the great mass of the population. However, the need will persist for the social engineers to resort to violence in order to silence all those people who may still be inclined to ask the glaringly obvious questions.

Men without Chests – C. S. Lewis' The Abolition of Man

Clive Staples Lewis (1898 –1963) was an outstanding Medieval and literary scholar, a best-selling author, and one of the most popular Christian apologists of the past 100 years. His "The Chronicles of Narnia" and "The Space Trilogy" have enjoyed uninterrupted popularity from the time of their publication to this day, with the former recently being brought successfully to the big screen. Lewis's works have been translated into more than 30 languages and have sold millions of copies worldwide. His remarkable ability to express complex philosophical ideas in simple terms accessible to the ordinary person underlined his true genius, and his influence in schools of philosophy around the world has continued to grow. Below is a paraphrase from his very short yet powerful book, "The Abolition of Man", that gives some indication of his thinking and his gifts of persuasion.

Society at large pays too little attention to the huge influence wielded by school textbooks. For that reason I want to introduce these lectures with reference to a smallish book on English written for pupils in the final years of their schooling.

It seems highly unlikely that the two writers were guilty of mischievous intentions, and in fact I am indebted to them and their publishing house for letting me have a free copy. Nonetheless, they will not enjoy what I have to say.

It is a most unfortunate situation I find myself in. While it is unpleasant having to castigate two presumably well-meaning teachers, it would be unethical to remain silent when I know only too well the damage the book is capable of doing. Hence, I will not disclose the names of the authors, and will merely refer to them as Gaius and Titius, and I will speak of their work as "The Green Book". But do not doubt for a moment that such a book exists – it is sitting on my bookshelf...

Gaius and Titius have come up with the clearly unexamined idea that courage and loyalty and justice might be instilled in pupils on a purely rational or evolutionary basis, using "modern" thinking.

If, for argument's sake, we concede that there might be grounds for justifying the virtues without any appeal to moral absolutes, the fact remains that such justification will not in itself make anyone virtuous.

The intellect needs properly controlled emotions in order to overcome the animal urges within us. With whom would you rather play cards – a man who questioned the validity of ethical standards, but who had been brought up in the belief that gentlemen never cheat, or a professor of ethics who had been raised by people who cheated all the time?

While rational arguments will do nothing to keep soldiers resolute in the trenches after three hours of artillery fire, even crudely stirred emotions about regimental pride or the honour of the country certainly will.

As Plato made clear, reason has to control the animal appetites by means of emotion. The head controls the stomach by means of the chest, the centre of character, where emotions are shaped by guidance and practice into sound sentiments. The heart, character, and sentiment are the civilising agents holding reason and desire to a proper course of action. It is what makes us human, because

183

through intellect we are simply spirit, and through appetite merely animal. "The Green Book" will give rise to men without chests.

Referring to the authors as intellectuals is a defensive ploy by the publisher to avert criticism. Gaius and Titius are in no way exceptional in their ability or passion to seek the truth. In fact, the perseverance and sense of intellectual honesty required for that distinction are irrefutably sentiments which the two authors would presumably treat with the same disdain as any other. Gaius and Titius are not distinguished by any breadth or depth of intellectual endeavour, but rather by the absence of any decent emotion. It is not that they have bigger heads, but rather that they have smaller chests.

The great irony of western civilisation is that we persist in calling for the very virtues that we are busy purging from the younger generations through our wilful irresponsibility. There is scarcely a magazine or newspaper being churned out today that does not insist that our society needs drive, self-sacrifice, and creativity. With an astonishing simple-mindedness, we surgically remove the organ, but still demand the function.

We destroy sentiment in the hearts of men, and continue to expect integrity and creativity from them. We openly ridicule honour and then profess to be outraged when we are confronted by treason.

One Word of Truth – Solzhenitsyn's Nobel Speech

Alexander Solzhenitsyn (1918 - 2008) was perhaps the greatest Russian writer of the twentieth century. He fought in the Red Army in World War II, and was twice decorated for bravery. However, his anti-Stalinist views led to his arrest and detention in the notorious Soviet Gulag system, and many of his novels and history books drew on his personal experiences. He was awarded the Nobel Prize for literature in 1970 but was unable to be present to accept the award. Four years later, he was again arrested and then expelled from the Soviet Union. His outspoken criticism of western decadence made him a controversial character during his exile, and he was often castigated by the same western media that had earlier lionized him while he was suffering his tribulations in the Soviet Union. He returned to Russia in 1990 to try and help in the rebuilding of the nation. Books like "One Day in the Life of Ivan Denisovich" and "The Gulag Archipelago" should be prescribed reading in our schools and universities. Even a brief reworking of a small part of his Nobel acceptance speech still conveys the wisdom of this great man.

With our savage, volatile, and wayward world on the brink of the abyss, what is the status and function of the writer?

There is simply no escape. From the moment one makes a commitment to the truth, the die is cast. The writer cannot simply be an arm-chair critic passing judgment on his compatriots. He shares the guilt for all the evil done in his homeland. When the blood of innocents is spilled in the streets of some foreign city by the armed forces of his country, the writer is tainted in the same way as everyone else is. When a loyal friend is strangled in his sleep, the writer cannot escape complicity. When the youth in his country prefer drunkenness and promiscuity to honest work, and are seduced by narcotics or make money through kidnapping, the stench is there on the writer's own breath.

It is my considered opinion that the literature of the world has the potential to enable humanity to understand itself better in this time of terror, regardless of the ideological demands of politicians and partisans. Great literature lets the people of one country grow through the distilled experiences of other countries. Different worldviews are then placed one beside another so that people can get an abbreviated yet accurate understanding of the history and culture of their fellow human beings from other lands. Inevitably they will have a sense of recognition and greater awareness of realities, as though the experience had been their own, and the likelihood of falling into the same old traps will thereby be reduced...

The responsibility of providing articulate and cogent criticism of incompetence on the part of their government rests squarely with the writers. Of course, in some countries there is no easier way to earn one's keep, and all except the indolent engage in it. But society needs to be chastened for its failings, whether for craven submission to authority, weak-minded complacency, the misguided antics of adolescents, or the spread of violent crime.

The objection will be raised that literature is impotent in the face of barbaric violence, but it must be remembered that violence can never succeed on its own. It always goes hand in hand with the lie. There is the most intimate relationship between them because violence needs to be concealed by untruth, and untruth needs violence to prop it up. Anyone who adopts violence as his policy is compelled to take untruth as his principle.

Initially, violence acts with bravado, but in time it becomes plain that people will not support it, and then it has to spin an ever-more intricate web of lies, to make itself more palatable. Violence does not necessarily need any active participation from citizens, but merely their loyalty to the lie.

The courageous response of the common man is to refuse to participate, and to reject the lies. If that is what is going happen, I will still have no part of it. However, the writer must do more: he has the power to defeat untruth. The arts have always triumphed over untruth, and when they do succeed, then the horror of violence is uncovered for the whole world to see – and the violence slowly withers away. That is the responsibility that all writers must accept – not to participate in disarmament protests or withdraw into cultural exile, but to stand firm in fighting the lie, wherever it might arise.

The most popular maxims in Russia are those that extol the truth. These ancient words of wisdom consistently bear witness to the tragic reality endured for so long by the people. A single word of truth is as valuable as the whole world.

Abuse of Language; Abuse of Power by Josef Pieper

Josef Pieper (1904 - 1997) was a leading German philosopher, whose views strongly reflected the influence of St. Thomas Aquinas and Plato. After studying philosophy, law, and sociology at the universities of Berlin and Münster, Pieper worked as a sociologist and a freelance writer, and later held the position of ordinary professor of philosophical anthropology at the University of Munster from 1950 to 1976. Thereafter, he continued to lecture at the university as professor emeritus until 1996. Pieper's thought has earned widespread respect throughout the academic world among agnostics and believers alike. The general reader will find that many of his short works on philosophical topics are well-worth dipping into and quite accessible, while "Leisure, the basis of culture" should be high on the reading lists of all government and business leaders. This review of a passage from "Abuse of language; abuse of power" shows how ancient wisdom throws light on a modern controversy.

Josef Pieper explains Plato's insight in seeing the smooth talk of the Sophists as the seductive illusion of the political process, enabling a fraudulent usurping of power from the legitimate authority. Pieper says that when public debate is abused by undermining truth, it becomes a valuable tool in the arsenal of the power-seekers and totalitarians. In the hands of unscrupulous politicians, the abuse of language is more commonly known as propaganda.

However, as Pieper points out, the use of propaganda is by no means confined to totalitarian regimes. It is in evidence wherever an ideological faction, a special interest, a lobby group, or any powerful agency employs the word as its weapon of choice. He notes that the word can be used to intimidate in many ways other than the threat of political persecution. Defamation, public ridicule, or reducing someone to the status of non-person, are all instances of how the word can wreak damage in the lives of people opposed to the power-seekers.

Pieper sees the common element as the degrading of language into an instrument of rape. That it does violence surreptitiously is demonstrated by Plato from his personal experience with the Sophists of his day. Plato's lesson says that the abuse of political power is intimately related to the corruption of the word, which actually provides the fertile ground in which it can grow. The surest way to discern the hidden potential for a totalitarian take-over is by being aware of the public misuse of language.

The humiliation of man by man through the acts of physical violence, like forced labour, torture, beatings, and murder, has its origin, when things appear more benign, in that almost indiscernible instant when the word loses its dignity. And the dignity of the word amounts to nothing more than the fact that it can do what nothing else can; that is, it can convey meaning based on reality, the way things actually are. When in the place of authentic reality a bogus reality is set up, then it becomes well-nigh impossible to discern the truth.

Pieper tells how Plato sweated over his philosophical labours for more than fifty years, always returning to the same question: what is it that makes the Sophists so dangerous? He finally wrote one last dialogue, "Sophist", in which he expounded on this fact that the Sophists set out to manufacture a fictitious reality. Pieper is not alone when he expresses his concerns that the Platonic nightmare has a terrifying relevance in the modern world.

Public opinion has been impoverished because people no longer know where to find the truth. Moreover, most people are not even inclined to look for it, deceived and manipulated as they are into going along with the fictitious reality created by the power-mongers through the corruption of language.

Pieper summarises Plato's position in three short statements: first, a meaningful human life requires, as far as possible, to be able to understand all things as they actually are, and to live and act in accordance with this reality, this truth; secondly, the potential of all people can only be brought to fruition by access and receptivity to truth, and society can only be sustained by a commitment to truth; and thirdly, the truth lives and grows naturally in human relationships where there is free and open communication.

Truth has to be promoted in dialogue, in discussion, in conversation, because its dwelling place is language, or the word.

A look at Vaclav Havel's speech on political correctness

Vaclav Havel (1936-2011) was a Czech writer, and politician. He became the last President of Czechoslovakia (1989 – 1992) and the first President of the Czech Republic (1993 – 2003). His literary works have been translated into many languages, and he was regarded as one of the leading advocates for liberal democracy around the world. Among the many other awards bestowed on him, he earned the US Presidential Medal of Freedom. Under the Communist regime in Czechoslovakia, Havel's political activism inevitably resulted in imprisonment, but it also gave him a growing international audience and recognition as the leader of the opposition in his country. As President of Czechoslovakia, he op- posed the split with Slovakia, and helped pave the way for membership of NATO and the European Union. This is the gist of what he said at one point in the speech at his inauguration.

My fellow citizens, for the past four decades you have been told different versions of the same old story from previous holders of this office. You have heard how well we were doing, and about our massive steel production, about the contentment of our peo- ple, about the integrity of the government, and about the glorious future opening up before us. I do not think that you elected me in order to hear more lies.

The country is not doing well at all. The prodigious potential of an innovative and energetic people is being wasted. Vast sectors of the economy are devoted to churning out items of little commercial value, while the necessary goods are ignored. A regime supposedly dedicated to the welfare of the workers exploits them ruthlessly. Our out-of-date economy squanders our meagre energy resources.

What was once one of the world's most effective education systems has fallen to number seventy-two in the world because of a lack of investment. The beautiful and fertile environment left to us by previous generations has been horribly polluted by us, and few parts of Europe are as bad. We have one of the highest adult mortality rates on the continent.

Let me share with you a personal revelation. On a recent flight to Bratislava, I took time out from official duties to look at our country from the air. Among the sights I took in were the extensive Slovnaft industrial complex and the sprawling Petr'alka housing estate nearby.

What I saw made it plain enough that no politician or bureaucrat of the past several decades could have looked out from their comfortable aircraft without being either deeply troubled or incurably cynical. The concrete reality was more damning than any statistical study could have been.

However, none of this addresses the real problem. Our most serious issue is the fact that we live in a moral atmosphere that has become pervasively corrupted. Our conscience has become seriously diseased because we became accustomed to making statements we ourselves did not believe. We became cynical, completely lacking in empathy, and wholly self-centred.

The meaning of essential concepts such as love, friendship, compassion, humility, and forgiveness was perverted or lost, and the more cold-hearted in our midst saw them simply as psychological aberrations. What relevance would such ancient relics have in the new age of technology?

Small indeed were the numbers of those still capable of denouncing the unlimited authority of the regime, and who demanded that the finest and most healthy food specially provided by elite farms for senior state officials should be given instead to school's, orphanages, and hospitals.

The cold and calculating ideology of the regime now removed from power looked on people as mere units of production, and nature as nothing more than raw material. This inhuman worldview misconstrued the very essence of man and nature and their intimate inter-dependence.

It regarded creative and free people as mere cogs in their ghastly machine, whose real purpose remained a mystery. That the deceitful regime finally managed to run itself into the ground was inevitable.

Our contaminated moral milieu is not confined to spoiled and indifferent state functionaries. It involves all of us. All of us bear some responsibility for what happened. More than victims, we were co-creators.

A look at *The Mystery of Capital* by Hernando de Soto

Hernando De Soto (born 1941) is a Peruvian economist named by Bill Clinton as "the world's greatest living economist". He has received similar praise from many of the World's leaders over the past twenty-five years, and his ideas have been strongly endorsed by the United Nations and luminaries from all sides of the socio-economic divide. He is the Founder and President of the Institute of Liberty and Democracy in Lima, an organisation rated by The Economist as the second most important think-tank in the world. He guided President Fujimoro's transformation of Peru, but his liberal ideas brought him into conflict with his former boss as well as the Shining Path guerrillas. He was the architect of the strategic plan that overturned Fujimoro's coup d'etat and set Peru back on the path to constitutional democracy. The following paraphrased excerpt from "The Mystery of Capital" gives one a useful summary of De Soto's thesis.

This book was written to show how the main obstacle standing in the way of the successful implementation of capitalism outside of the West is the inability to generate capital. Capital fuels the productivity of labour and is indisputably the most effective means of producing prosperity. Without capital the free market would not exist; progress is built on it. Sadly, it is also the essential element that Third World countries seem incapable of generating on their own, regardless of all the initiative and effort their people pour into the other activities that contribute to the setting up of a capitalist system.

Over many years, a huge catalogue of data was compiled by a body of professional researchers studying scores of neighbourhoods and farms in Asia, Africa, the Middle East, and Latin America. This body of research makes it clear for all to see that a majority of poor people in Third World countries are already in possession of the assets they require to participate in a capitalist economy. Indeed, there are no poor countries where the economically-marginalised people do not have savings.

In fact, the value of savings these people have accumulated over the years is staggering, amounting to forty times the value of all the foreign aid actually transferred worldwide since 1945. Taking Egypt as an example, we find that the wealth of the poor is fifty-five times greater than the value of all direct overseas investment ever made, which includes huge projects like the Suez Canal and the Aswan Dam.

Haiti is the most impoverished country in the western hemisphere, yet the poor have assets worth more than all foreign investment transferred there since independence in 1804. Even if the United States foreign aid outlay was to meet the 0.7 percent of national income proposed by the UN, the world's wealthiest country would still only match the value of assets already held by the poor after another 150 years of giving aid.

Regrettably, possession of these assets is not guaranteed by law. There are homes erected on land where ownership rights are open to dispute, businesses that have no real legal definition of rights and responsibilities, and manufacturing enterprises all but hidden from potential investors. An absence of documentation prevents these resources from being converted into capital, and they remain locked in confined localities where a sense of community and trust enables trading to be carried on. Hence these assets can never be used as collateral for loans or as investment opportunities.

This is completely at odds with the capitalist system developed in the West. There, the legal status of each piece of real estate, each building, each item of equipment, each stock of produce or manufactured goods, is documented and defined, providing certifiable evidence for the all-embracing process that encapsulates all these assets in the economic life of the country.

This representational system enables resources to have additional value over and above their physical properties and the price they fetch. They can most obviously be used to secure loans or investments, and in fact, in the United States, the most common way of financing a new business venture is to take out a mortgage on one's home.

This system also makes available as a matter of public record all data on the credit history of individuals and organisations, and established addresses for invoicing and tax purposes. And of course, tax enables the development of infrastructure and public utilities. The hard assets are also used to create securities which are, in turn, able to generate further economic activity.

Sadly, Third World countries do not possess the formal property rights established by this legal documentation process. Instead, the poor people in those countries are confronted by a jungle of bureaucratic complexity and corruption that soon dampens all enthusiasm for entrepreneurship.

Social trends, in Barzun's *From Dawn to Decadence*

Jacques Barzun (1907 –2008) was one of the great teachers and literary and cultural scholars of the past century. Born in France, Barzun grew up in America. He received a PhD from Columbia, and taught there for many years. The combined lectures he gave with the equally famous Lionel Trilling were from all accounts learning experiences to be savoured for a lifetime. His reputation as a teacher was legendary, and "Begin Here" is a book on education that would be hard to beat for sheer practical wisdom. We are fortunate to have so many of his books available, and all have the power to teach new generations with the same insight and inspiration that encouraged earlier ones. For those interested in culture and the significance of literature in particular, I would recommend "The House of Intellect", "The Culture we Deserve", and "Classic, Romantic, and Modern". Barzun was 93 years old when he completed the remarkable history, "From Dawn to Decadence", and it is a work of staggering erudition and wisdom. Already regarded as a classic, it is one of those books a person can open on any page at random, and be certain of coming away better educated. One only hopes that the current generation of history teachers will avail themselves of the richly informative and entertaining content of this timely review of modern civilisation. The following look at a passage out of "From Dawn to Decadence" is replete in lessons about ourselves and our culture.

Jacques Barzun poses the question as to what the contents of Western culture are, and *From Dawn to Decadence* traces in broad strokes the revolution of art, science, religion, philosophy, and social ideas over the past half millennium. His intention is to show that in this long era Western civilisation produced ideas and institutions that were radically different from the rest of the world, and which composed a unity of remarkable diversity.

Barzun sees the West as "the mongrel civilisation par excellence", since it has taken much of its culture from other civilisations, and continual cross-pollination and the constant conflict of ideas has served it well.

For all the diversity and conflict, the West has still moved inexorably towards the achievement of certain unifying goals, and ironically, the current decline of the West is intimately related to these goals. This can be readily seen in the impasse around some key cultural issues: nationalism versus cosmopolitanism; individualism versus community; high culture versus pop culture and kitsch; definite moral standards versus moral relativism; and religious belief versus nihilism.

Barzun points to the array of rights exercised by the individual in an atmosphere of growing licence, and the extension of rights in all directions: illegal immigrants, children, criminals, plants, and animals. This universal freedom is a central feature of the West, "perhaps the most characteristic of all" according to Barzun. Of course, it does demand increasing regulation to prevent one freedom infringing another.

He identifies primitivism as a related theme in Western culture. This yearning to be free of the complexities of a progressive civilisation recurs throughout the half millennium. It helps drive the Protestant Reformation; then it re-emerges as the cult of the Noble Savage, long enough before Rousseau's time to prove that it was not his idea. The life of the savage is seen as healthier, more ethical, and less stressed than that of civilised man with all its conniving and deceit.

Primitivism re-emerges in the late 18th century, again in the 19th, and again in the Flower Power communes of the 1960s, when young people came to believe that a superficially defined "love" was the panacea for all social ills.

In Barzun's mind, there can be no abrupt and absolute end to the cultural process, and he emphasises that "decadence" simply means "falling off". It does not necessarily suggest that people who live at the time experience a loss of energy, ability, or morality, and in fact our current world is highly active and focussed on many momentous challenges. But in all this there is a distinct restlessness because people have no clear vision of the future they must pursue.

Western culture, in effect, confronts the loss of possibility, and therefore of hope. Art and life seem barren, and institutions merely go through the motions. People become frustrated with what feels like life on a treadmill. Boredom and apathy are cultural time-bombs.

Barzun anticipates the question of how the historian can discern when decadence afflicts a culture. He believes that it is when there is an open admission of despair, and people seek wildly for something new to believe in. The proliferation of cults, like Yoga, transcendental meditation, and the Moonies, highlight this response, with some even embracing group suicide.

Secular minds reject the faith option, but set up environmental, political, or social religions, often violent, in its place: the anti-nuclear movement, climate change, anti-abortion activism, eco-extremism, the organic foods lobby, and opposition to science and technology.

According to Barzun, it is primitivism that drives all of these flourishing movements.

A look at *Truth and Tolerance* by Pope Benedict XVI

Joseph Alois Ratzinger (1927 -) was elected as Bishop of Rome follow-ing the death of Pope John Paul II in 2005. He had been Prefect of the Congregation for the Doctrine of the Faith in Rome for many years, working closely with his predecessor to rejuvenate the Church once more. A prolific writer and one of the leading theologians of the age, Benedict has done much to defuse the unbalanced media scare-mongering that accompanied his election, building his Pontificate on the premise of his first encyclical "God is Love", and reaching out to other faiths in open dialogue. The paraphrase below from his book, "Truth and Tolerance", gives some idea of his philosophical standpoint on freedom and truth.

Pope Benedict says that in maintaining our Enlightenment heri-tage, three key points need clarification:

1. The idea of freedom is misunderstood when it is seen merely as a continual loosening of standards of behaviour, and the inexora-ble expansion of individual freedom in the direction of the ulti-mate removal of all constraints. Genuine freedom can only relate to the truth of what we actually are, corresponding to our human nature; if it does not, then it leads to dishonesty and self-

destruction. Humans are beings who exist in "being-from, being-with, and being-for" other people, which means freedom is only possible "in an ordered co-existence of freedoms". Law does not oppose freedom, but actually makes it possible.

Freedom is not the eradication of law and standards, but rather the perfection of ourselves and our standards, as individuals and in community, so that the co-existence of freedoms implied by human nature may be fully achieved.

2. There is a second consequence arising out of the reality of human nature. The absolutely ideal form of society will never be achieved in human history, and perfect freedom for all is beyond us in this world. Human beings are limited beings and are always moving on. The obvious maladies of the socialist system and the inadequacies of the liberal state drove Szczypiorski to wonder despairingly whether there was a right way at all. We can now say with some certainty that socio-political perfection is something we will never achieve. And it is also fair to say that anyone who claims to have the ideal model is being untruthful.

This does not mean that belief in progress is entirely erroneous. But the myth of a free world of the future where there will be no struggle, sacrifice, or suffering is deceitful. Human limitations mean we can only ever create relative social systems that are only relatively good and just. But this is precisely what urges us to strive to get as near as possible to perfection. Everything else, every ideological promise of the perfect society within history, does not free us, but enslaves us instead.

That is why the seductive myth around the ideas of change and revolution must be demythologised. Change is not necessarily good – its goodness or badness is determined by its content and how it impacts on other things. The argument that proclaims that the key challenge in the quest for freedom is in changing the world is simply false. Benedict emphasises that there has always been, and will always be, both progress and regress in history.

3. The third point is that the Enlightenment dream of autonomous and self-sufficient human reason has proved to be a mirage. Human reason needs guidance from the great religious traditions, even though it must examine each of those traditions critically. The corruption of religion is the most malignant illness of the human spirit, and can be found in all religions. However, it arises in precisely those areas where faith is rejected and relative goods are given an absolute value.

The atheist totalitarian regimes of our era are ugly examples of religious fervour cut adrift from its proper focus, and the disease of the human spirit that results from this.

Freedom is not promoted by the denial of the existence of God; it is actually robbed of its foundation and becomes disfigured. To reject the profound religious traditions of humanity is to walk away from truth. Moreover, morality cannot be purely philosophical. It cannot do without the concept of God and it cannot do without the concept of truth for a being that has an ethical nature.

Benedict concludes: "If there is no truth about man, then he has no freedom. Only the truth makes us free."

Appendix A – some essential reading

1. W. Churchill – A History of the English Speaking Peoples

2. Robin Lane Fox – The Classical World

3. Christopher Dawson – The Making of Europe

4. Jean Gimpel – The Medieval Machine

5. Rodney Stark – God's Battalions

6. Jacques Barzun – From Dawn to Decadence

7. Simon Schama – Citizens

8. Bruce Catton – This Hallowed Ground

9. Niall Ferguson – Empire

10. Paul Johnson – A History of the American People

11. Paul Johnson – Modern Times

12. Michael Burleigh – The Third Reich

13. Neil Postman – Amusing Ourselves to Death

14. Christopher Lasch – The Culture of Narcissism

15. Jonathan Rose – The Intellectual Life of the British Working Classes

Appendix B – 75 Masterpieces to Contemplate

1. *The Arnolfini Portrait* – Jan van Eyck
2. *Portrait of a Man* – Antonello da Messina
3. *Lorenzo de Medici* – Andrea del Verrocchio
4. *The Birth of the Virgin* – Domenico Ghirlandaio
5. *Primavera* – Sandro Botticelli
6. *Mona Lisa* – Leonardo da Vinci
7. *The Sistine Chapel* – Michelangelo
8. *The School of Athens* – Raphael
9. *Portrait of Andrea Doria* – Sebastiano del Piombo
10. *Venus of Urbino* – Titian
11. *The Last Supper* – Jacopo Robusti Tintoretto
12. *The Marriage Feast at Cana* – Paolo Veronese
13. *Children's Games* – Pieter Bruegel the Elder
14. *Queen Mary I* – Anthonis Mor
15. *Self-Portrait* – Albrecht Durer
16. *The Ambassadors* – Hans Holbein
17. *Portrait Bust of Cosimo I de Medici* – Benvenuto Cellini
18. *The Rape of a Sabine* – Giambologna
19. *View of Toledo* – El Greco
20. *Supper at Emmaus* – Caravaggio
21. *The Payment of Taxes* – Georges de La Tour
22. *Peasant Family in an Interior* – Le Nain
23. *Louis XVI* – Hyacinthe Rigaud
24. *Quince, Cabbage, Melon, and Cucumber* – Juan Sanchez Cotan
25. *An Old Woman Cooking Eggs* – Velazquez
26. *The Descent from the Cross* – Rubens
27. *Lord John and Lord Bernard Stuart* – Anthony van Dyck

28. *The Laughing Cavalier* – Frans Hals

29. *Company Mascot* – Rembrandt

30. *The Milkmaid* – Jan Vermeer

31. *Still Life with Food and Drink* – Willem Claesz Heda

32. *Madame de Pompadour* – Francois Boucher

33. *Return of the Bucintoro on Ascension Day* – Canaletto

34. *Marriage a la Mode: The Toilette* – William Hogarth

35. *The Ladies Waldegrave* – Joshua Reynolds

36. *Mr. and Mrs. Andrews* – Gainsborough

37. *An Experiment on a Bird in the Air Pump* – Joseph Wright

38. *Sir Walter Scott* – Henry Raeburn

39. *The Death of Marat* – Jacques-Louis David

40. *Napoleon Visits the Plague-Stricken at Jaffa* – Antoine Jean Gros

41. *The Declaration of Independence* – John Trumbull

42. *The Raft of the Medusa* – Gericault

43. *Liberty Leading the People* – Delacroix

44. *The Third of May 1808* – Goya

45. *The Hay Wain* – Constable

46. *The Fighting Temeraire* – Turner

47. *The Oregon Trail* – Albert Bierstadt

48. *The Angelus* – Jean-Francois Millet

49. *The Zaporozhye Cossacks* – Ilya Repin

50. *Proserpine* – Dante Gabriel Rossetti

51. *A Roman Slave Market* – Jean-Leon Gerome

52. *A Bar at the Folies-Bergere* – Manet

53. *The Waterlily Pond* – Monet

54. *The Luncheon of the Boating Party* – Renoir

55. *In a Café, or Absinthe* – Degas

56. *Dance at the Moulin Rouge* – Toulouse-Lautrec

57. *The Thinker* – Rodin

58. *Sunday Afternoon on the Island of La Grande Jatte* – Seurat

59. *In Time of Peril* – Edmund Blair Leighton

60. *Card Players* – Cezanne

61. *Woman with a Flower* – Gauguin

62. *The Starry Night* – van Gogh

63. *The Gross Clinic* – Thomas Eakins

64. *View of Toledo* – El Greco

65. *Red and Black – the Fan* – Whistler

66. *The Sadness of the King* – Matisse

67. *March of the Weavers* – Kathe Kollwitz

68. *Judith* – Gustav Klimt

69. *Le Portugais* – Georges Braque

70. *Guernica* – Picasso

71. *La Ville de Paris* – Robert Delaunay

72. *A Battery Shelled* – Wyndham Lewis

73. *Nude with Necklace* – Modigliani

74. *Christ of St. John of the Cross* – Dali

75. *Autumn Rhythm* – Jackson Pollock

Appendix C – 25 pieces of music to spend time with

1. *Canon in D* – Johann Pachelbel
2. *Trumpet Voluntary* – Jeremiah Clarke
3. *Jesu, Joy of Man's Desiring* – Johann Sebastian Bach
4. *The Brandenburg Concerto* – Johann Sebastian Bach
5. *Symphony 43 in F major* – Wolfgang Amadeus Mozart
6. *Champagne Aria* – Wolfgang Amadeus Mozart
7. *Largo* – George Frideric Handel
8. *Cello Concerto* – Franz Joseph Haydn
9. *Polonaise in A Major* – Frederic Chopin
10. *La Traviata* – Giuseppe Verdi
11. *Moonlight Sonata* – Ludwig von Beethoven
12. *Sonata No. 8 Pathetique* – Ludwig von Beethoven
13. *Serenade* – Franz Schubert
14. *Carmen – Prelude to Act I* – Georges Bizet
15. *Violin Concerto* – Felix Mendelssohn
16. *Liebestraum* – Franz Liszt
17. *Ride of the Valkyries* – Richard Wagner
18. *The 1812 Overture* – Peter Ilyich Tchaikovsky
19. *Piano Concerto No. 1* – Peter Ilyich Tchaikovsky
20. *In the Hall of the Mountain King* – Edvard Grieg
21. *Clair de Lune* – Claude Debussy
22. *Rhapsody in Blue* – George Gershwin
23. *Land of Hope and Glory* – Edward William Elgar
24. *Festliche Hymne* – Jean Sibelius
25. *Concierto de Aranjuez* – Joachim Rodrigo

Appendix D – 25 movies and documentaries to enjoy

1. Julius Caesar (Director Joseph L Mankiewicz)
2. Becket
3. The Mission
4. A Man for All Seasons
5. Macbeth (Ian McKellan, Judi Dench, Royal Shakespeare Co.)
6. Moliere
7. Amadeus
8. Barry Lyndon
9. Master and Commander
10. The Duellists
11. Waterloo
12. Pride and Prejudice
13. Amazing Grace
14. Gettysburg
15. Cinderella Man
16. The Gathering Storm
17. Schindler's List
18. To kill a mockingbird
19. Hotel Rwanda
20. Blood Diamond
21. The Lives of Others
22. The Last Emperor
23. Empire of the Sun
24. The Civil War by Ken Burns
25. History of England by Simon Schama